D0152070

Working with Millennials

Working with Millennials

Using Emotional Intelligence and Strategic Compassion to Motivate the Next Generation of Leaders

Marc Robertson

Foreword by Adam Lichtl

PROPERTY OF
SOUTH UNIVERSITY LIBRARY
NOVI CAMPUS
NOVI, MI
248-675-0242

An Imprint of ABC-CLIO, LLC
Santa Barbara, California • Denver, Colorado

Baker College of Clinton Twp Library

Copyright © 2016 by Marc Robertson

All rights reserved. No part of this publication may be reproduced, stored in a retrieval system, or transmitted, in any form or by any means, electronic, mechanical, photocopying, recording, or otherwise, except for the inclusion of brief quotations in a review, without prior permission in writing from the publisher.

Library of Congress Cataloging-in-Publication Data

Names: Robertson, Marc (Marc Allen), author.
Title: Working with millennials : using emotional intelligence and strategic compassion to motivate the next generation of leaders / Marc Robertson ; foreword by Adam Lichtl.
Description: Santa Barbara, California : Praeger, [2016] | Includes bibliographical references and index.
Identifiers: LCCN 2015036940 | ISBN 9781440844126 (alk. paper) | ISBN 9781440844133 (ebk)
Subjects: LCSH: Generation Y—Employment. | Intergenerational relations. | Conflict of generations in the workplace. | Emotional intelligence. | Leadership. | Personnel management.
Classification: LCC HF5549.5.C75 R63 2016 | DDC 658.3/14—dc23 LC record available at http://lccn.loc.gov/2015036940

ISBN: 978-1-4408-4412-6
EISBN: 978-1-4408-4413-3

20 19 18 17 16 1 2 3 4 5

This book is also available on the World Wide Web as an eBook.
Visit www.abc-clio.com for details.

Praeger
An Imprint of ABC-CLIO, LLC

ABC-CLIO, LLC
130 Cremona Drive, P.O. Box 1911
Santa Barbara, California 93116-1911

This book is printed on acid-free paper ∞

Manufactured in the United States of America

This book is dedicated to
Daisaku Ikeda, who inspires me daily.

Contents

Foreword *by Adam Lichtl* ix

Acknowledgments xiii

Introduction xv

Chapter 1. You Don't Have to Be an Expert 1
Increase Productivity by Increasing EQ

Chapter 2. The Privilege of Leadership 13
The Simultaneity of Cause and Effect

Chapter 3. Getting Out of Your Own Way 23
Emotional Triggers and Building a Solid Self

Chapter 4. People Are Your Resources 33
Focus on Others to Get What You Want

Chapter 5. The Notion of Strategic Compassion 41
Building Trust and Creating Value through an Enlightened Leadership

Chapter 6. There's No Such Thing as a Safe Place 49
The Difference between Leading and Managing

Chapter 7. Getting Gold Out of Them 63
They Will Kill for You if You Demonstrate Real Concern

Chapter 8. Dealing with Pushback 73
The Art of War in Contemporary Business

Chapter 9. How to Lead Meetings 83
Never Engage without a Plan

Chapter 10. Creating the Culture You Want 95
And Breaking Down the One You Don't Want

Chapter 11. Becoming the Complete Leader 105
The Art of Communication

Chapter 12. Why Compassionate Leadership Is in Your Self-Interest 115

Appendix: Millennial Generation Facts and Figures 125

Index 127

Foreword

Rule number one of business is that you must adapt to survive. This applies not only to market strategies or supply chain logistics, but also to the very way you motivate and lead your team. As technical innovation continues to dominate the marketplace, more and more enterprise value is being allocated to the minds that generate those ideas. We live in a society of "knowledge workers," and companies are realizing their most valuable asset is their people.

At the same time, there is a growing disconnect between the younger workforce and the people who manage them. The outdated practice of management by positional authority, effective when job mobility was limited, is crumbling before the newer, more effective, technique of "strategic compassion." By blending emotional intelligence with technical acumen, the most effective leaders out there are building lasting, productive teams by creating a healthy environment based on collaboration, not intimidation.

The Millennials (those born between 1980 and 2000) have less loyalty to their jobs than older workers. In 2014, the Bureau of Labor Statistics reported that the median tenure, or number of years with their current employer, for wage and salary workers was 3.0 years for workers aged 25–34. For workers aged 55–64, the median tenure was 10.4 years, more than three times that of the Millennial workers.[1] Three years is about the time needed to recruit, vet, train, and integrate a highly productive person into your organization. Right when you're starting to see a return on your investment, if your environment is toxic, they're likely halfway out the door looking for their next opportunity. As the economy strengthens, retention only gets harder.

Many businesses have adopted a policy of "get 'em young, burn 'em out," embracing high turnover rates. In the short term, this strategy is seductive as it keeps wages low and exploits a seemingly bottomless pool of energetic young people looking for work experience. However, this approach is untenable in the long term. As a constant stream of young, enthusiastic but inexperienced people are coming in your front door, you're losing a constant stream of more experienced workers carrying your organization's culture and intellectual property in their heads. Your top performers are the most employable, and often the first to leave. They're also the ones you rely on to screen your next candidates, train your new hires, and mentor your junior employees. Every quality person a company lets slip through its fingers erodes that organization's ability to compete in the marketplace.

If direct compensation is not enough to retain your Millennial talent, then what is? The three major ingredients for a satisfied employee are clear expectations, support, and appreciation. Setting out not only what is expected, but also where they can expect to be in two years, provides a clear path forward. This in turn means that Millennials looking for growth and change can find that within your organization, not outside of it. Trust is the cornerstone of good communication. You can't help an employee reach his or her goals if you don't know what those are, and they won't share those with someone they don't trust. Integrity in dealing with other people is a universal necessity in business, but is not sufficient to build trust. For someone to know you have their back, you have to show them constant and meaningful support. Being honest with someone is expected, but you must go beyond this—actively giving them the training and encouragement they need to succeed. And when they do succeed, be right there with them, showing them that you recognize and appreciate their contribution.

This collaborative approach is a potent form of leadership, but requires a dramatic shift in thinking from the typical, but increasingly ineffective, command-and-control approach to management. Shifting emphasis from authority and reporting, to emotional intelligence and strategic compassion, is not an easy process for most people. However, Marc Robertson uses thousands of hours of his coaching to lay out in this book the exact steps you need to take to greatly improve the way you lead and manage. This book will walk you through the specific actionable changes you can implement in your organization, what impact you can expect those changes to make, and how to deal with the bumps along the way. As you head down this new road, you'll find yourself at the helm of a much more productive, energized, and healthy organization. And as your team's culture strengthens and the gap between you and your competition widens, the word will get out. Soon enough, you'll find that your competition's top performers will be knocking on your door.

—Adam Lichtl, Former Director of Research, SpaceX

NOTE

1. Bureau of Labor Statistics, Employee Tenure News Release, September 18, 2014, http://www.bls.gov/news.release/archives/tenure_09182014.htm.

Acknowledgments

I'd like to thank the following individuals, without whom this book could not have been written:

John Moshay, for encouraging me to set forth in writing what I've learned over many years of coaching highly successful individuals.

Jeff Ourvan, my literary agent, for guiding and helping me through the writing, editing, and publishing process.

Special thanks to Isabel Aldeguer MD for her loving push, and Shinji Ishibashi, Michelle Suzuki, Mark Iwanowski, Felicia Zigman and Adam Lichtl for their many ideas and steadfast support.

Finally, everyone with whom I have had the privilege of working as a coach. You are the ones that tackled the issues you were faced with and had the courage to change and grow. It has been an honor, and each of you makes me very proud.

Introduction

Some years ago, I walked into a venerable advertising company and saw nothing but waves of young people under the age of 30. I had been recruited by the only two individuals in office suites that I was sure were a bit older—the CEO and COO of the firm. What they wanted from me was help in coaching *them*—the young people on the floor, the leading edge of what had already been dubbed the Millennial generation. Everyone is so young but so talented they told me. They want to take on responsibilities very fast, they don't like it when we impose various work constrictions, they're a little self-centered—and, these bosses emphasized, "we don't want any of them to leave."

Now I'm old enough to remember what ad agencies used to look like—guys, just like in "Mad Men," walking arrogantly down the halls in their designer suits and into their individual offices, their female secretaries hovering just outside.

But here, even the managers were under 30. And there were hardly any private offices, no secretarial pods—rather most everyone was congregated in a large bullpen, some in cubicles, some with desks pushed together and organized by group or department. Needless to say, no one here would be inviting me out for two-martini lunches. Instead, lunch was ordered in, and these Millennials worked straight through at their desks. People were literally on top of each other—and it wasn't some call center, it was a real office, with directors, managers, and workers all busily engaged in their jobs. Imagine that.

This was terrific, I thought. I had no frame of reference to anything like this from back when I started my career, but here the office was set up precisely to promote communications and team building. Everyone knew everything—there was some separation but not much. And I thought it was cool—I thought it was *unity*. Here, in an open, shared environment, it's pretty easy to deduce that you can't be a jerk and expect to survive. Everyone would be immediately exposed.

Still, honestly, at the time I felt like a stranger in a strange land. There's nothing older than advertising, and suddenly now everything had changed.

Millennials, as I've come to now know very well, are a different bunch as compared to their parents—the baby boomers—that preceded them. They're driven, they want to move up, they probably do feel too entitled, they don't like to give up what they started, they work long hours, they don't seek interpersonal confrontations, they prefer flexible hours, and they're inclined to move in packs. Yes, they do like working in groups—that's why offices today are arranged the way they are—and although like anyone else they require guidance and mentoring, they sometimes make the mistake of not asking for it. Millennials don't "appreciate" diversity—it's more like they don't even notice something so normal and, relative to their experiences, banal.

Year after year, as I worked at startups and traditional firms absorbing majorities of Millennial workers, I saw companies grow as fast as I've ever seen any company expand—doubling in size at times in as little as three months. I'm thinking to myself, this really works. But do they ever take time off for themselves?

Millennials are a fascinating group—unlike the boomers, it's as if they've collectively decided not to take on their parents' problems. Boomers, all the way back to when they were hippies, always felt some burden to straighten something out—whether it was the Vietnam War, women's rights, or American culture in general. Millennials, on the other hand, are quite happy to want to do things their own way; they're not particularly caring for or building on what their parents did. They're instead more fascinated by their own ideas. And they want to cross-pollinate those ideas with other like-minded Millennials.

Work hours today are structured much differently than they were even 10 years ago. At Hulu, for example, there's a terrific guy named Ben Richardson who is the assistant to the executive I coach there. Ben manages the calendars for my coaching sessions at their offices. I do some coaching over there on occasion, and usually on Sunday nights I'll set up my conference room needs for later in the week. So I e-mailed him with my preferred times late one Sunday night—and to my surprise I got an immediate response. He was working.

The Millennials have collectively established a sort of 24/7 ecosystem in which work gets accomplished at all hours. They might at times wander in late to the office, or take off in the afternoons to go to a gym, or maybe pick up a kid from school, but then they'll make up the work later in the day—and corporations today, of course, are perfectly fine in general with such flexible work patterns. The problem that Millennials have, interestingly, isn't that they take advantage of their freedoms to leave work at all hours. Instead, a lot of them end up overworking and not taking care of themselves—they're doing too much work. At times I've had to coach young people about making room for their personal lives. Contrary to some studies or general anecdotal observations, Millennials—at least the employed ones—are far from lazy people.

Millennial-generation managers and employees—those ages 18–35—have transformed and are continuing to change the face of business in America. Within 10 years, it's estimated, greater than 70 percent of the U.S. workforce will be of Millennial age.

More than any other generation, they don't conform to the traditional ways of doing things. Rather than passively taking orders, they thirst for engagement, expect to be part of a team, and want to be in on the action. They assume work will be, at least sometimes, fun. And they want to be trained and tasked with meaningful assignments—unlike past generations, they're not devoted to the corporation as much as they are to the product or service that's provided.

This book will show you how both to work with Millennials but also succeed in the business environments of the 21st century that have undoubtedly already been transformed by our now youngest adult generation.

With the goal of encouraging business leaders to adapt seamlessly to the demands of a new workplace, in particular you'll see emphasized here the importance of emotional intelligence (EQ) and development of leadership skills:

- how to coach others to resolve immediate conflicts between management and their teams;
- how to transform toxic work environments into collaborative and productive ones;
- how to turn difficult, impatient, and angry managers who have lost the trust and confidence of their staffs into leaders who earn the trust and respect of their reports;
- how to create an open communication style that, in turn, will develop a culture that creates trust, unity, and a supportive work environment; and, most importantly,
- how to build true leaders for the future.

Based on a Buddhist-related concept I've dubbed strategic compassion, this book trains and teaches new leaders—particularly our so-called

Millennials—the leadership skills needed to build the confidence that will enable them to immediately earn the trust and respect of their teams. The result is improved productivity through individual growth and long-term interdepartmental cooperation.

It's easy to succumb to your emotional triggers and shout at someone and stamp your feet if you don't get your way. But that model of doing business, in this generation, is long dead. Instead, the most successful business leaders of the future will be, of course, daring and intelligent—that will never change—but they'll also be the ones who come to develop their inner strengths.

This is not an easy task—if you want to remain an individual contributor in your company I understand completely. If you want to simply manage and be happy with that, that's fine too. Every firm needs capable managers. But being a leader in the Millennial age demands extra effort and dedication, passion, and most importantly requires you to care about other people in a genuine way. Leadership is service. If you can't do this, you can't lead. If you're willing to try, the rewards can be limitless. And by this I mean in the realms of monetary, emotional, and lifelong personal satisfaction.

There is an opportunity at this time in corporate America to lead. I say this because I also know that there's a gaping hole in most corporations with respect to finding the people who are equipped to lead this generation.

And it's a finite window of time. Moreover, there's also a limited period during which someone's career can develop. If you're not invested now, if you're not seriously adapting your management techniques today, you'll have to undue your bad habits later on.

New corporate leadership, one based on the ethos of strategic compassion described in these pages, will make the difference in the next five years.

Don't avoid it, but rather engage now—it's not only coming, but in some cases it's already here.

Chapter 1

You Don't Have to Be an Expert

Increase Productivity by Increasing EQ

This is a career book—not a textbook or a philosophical tome about how to do business. This book is all about improving your leadership skills and getting results. It is a blueprint both for young people who want to take responsibility and grow and for those having difficulties in their organizations. It provides the keys to improve your current status, or evolve into a higher position. It's the toolbox to prepare you for your next great gig—or to do much better in the one you have and become happier, wealthier, and more satisfied as part of the process.

More than anything today, in our so-called Millennial age, people in management positions, or in any corporate setting, will need to nurture the abilities to listen to and empathize with coworkers, supervisors, and employees. The old ways of managing—through fear and intimidation—don't work. Those prescriptions have expired. Strength in business, rather, now derives more from self-control rather than the knack for creating terror in others. Those with the highest emotional intelligence quotient (EQ) insure the greatest productivity and growth.

Emotional intelligence is the ability to accurately and effectively monitor not only your emotions but the emotions of others as well. A high-EQ performer will discriminate between different behaviors and consciously use that information to guide his or her thinking and actions. EQ encompasses a wide array of skills and characteristics that drive leadership performances. Studies have shown that people with high EQ have greater mental health, exemplary job performances, and more potent leadership skills. Most importantly, leadership acumen and a high EQ (as opposed, for example, to a high IQ) is available to each of us. There are a million good managers, but only a handful of great leaders. And a high EQ is the difference between whether you're a manager or a leader.

A while ago I had an opportunity to travel to Europe on Virgin Atlantic. I found one steward on the flight to be particularly friendly and helpful, and so I struck up a conversation with him about why he appeared so happy at work. He told me that Virgin Atlantic was a terrific employer. He then explained to me that he almost left the company for another airline because the competitor offered much better pay and incentives. In fact, he had already accepted the other job. When he told his boss at Virgin Atlantic that he was jumping to a different airline, the supervisor understood his reasons for doing so. However, that manager must have reported the steward's decision up the line, because shortly thereafter the steward received a phone call from none other than Richard Branson—the Virgin Atlantic founder. Now Branson is a very busy guy, with lots of interests, and Virgin Atlantic is a major employer with several thousand workers worldwide. So Branson told the steward that he had heard he's an excellent worker and asked him why he decided to leave. The steward explained that he has a young family and needed the extra money that the competing airline offered. Interestingly, Branson didn't offer to match the compensation. Instead, he was straight with the steward—he told him that he couldn't pay him the compensation he had been offered but that he would provide a reasonable raise along with his gratitude for the good job the steward had done and his hope that a man like him would stay with the Virgin Atlantic family. The steward was so impressed by this approach that he told Branson he'd stay. And, at the time I spoke with him, he told me that he had no regrets whatsoever. Clearly, Branson practices a high-EQ leadership approach.

Leaders who listen to and empathize with coworkers and employees increase productivity, efficiency, and performance (PEP); diminish turnover; and create an environment that encourages people to want to work hard and do well. Specific components of EQ include self-awareness; self-management, and the flexibility to adapt to changing situations and obstacles; integrity, honesty, and trustworthiness; optimism; a drive to both learn and achieve; social competence; empathy and insight, and the ability to understand other perspectives; and conflict management skills based on respect for others and the ability to collaborate.

What kind of environment do you want to work in? Year after year studies are conducted. The findings show that the established and primary reason that people go to work is not to make money but to be acknowledged and appreciated. Everyone wants to be treated the same way—with consideration and respect. Effective leadership requires both a clever head *and* an empathetic heart. The notion of a successful toxic manager is a myth. Strong managers are not forged by virtue of shouting but instead through logic and consideration. I'm not simply suggesting that being a nice person is good for business—rather, it's that open and humanistic managers who master the art of listening to their employees show real-world profitability and results and grow themselves.

The first step is to put yourself in the other person's shoes. This is perhaps the most critical lesson in this new, Millennial era of business leadership: before doing anything, or making any decision, *you* have to grow and develop the ability to put your own wants and needs aside long enough to look at the world through *their* eyes. Part of the work of being a leader is to get past one's self. So, you ask, how do I do this?

Sometimes this is as simple as asking your workers or coworkers how they're doing. It's about stripping away anxiety and breaking down barriers. Just as a body affects the shadow, when you change your behavior, the results will change. It's both this simple and that hard. You may still have to increase pressure on those working for you, but there's alternatively a positive and a threatening way of how to do it.

In particular, you need to train people in a humanistic and open environment when you're first starting a new company or department. If you don't, then in quick order, and if the company or department survives, you'll end up in a silent work environment consumed with self-interest. And then you'll have to face the very difficult task of trying to undo a negative workplace culture. It's much more effective to get it right from the beginning.

Positive pressure on workers and coworkers engages an individual as an integral part of team and therefore nurtures responsibility. You're telling the person working with you that you believe in him or her. And when you ask the employee to perform some seemingly impossible task he or she will be motivated to want to try, because the underlying message is that you believe that he or she can do it. By vesting someone with such responsibility, and treating him or her with respect, you're saying that you put that person on the team and surrounded them with capable people because you believe that he or she can do it. They get it that you believe that they will do their best not to fail.

Of course there's always a risk when you push the envelope in this way. So when you do you need to have the courage to support those under pressure. What I mean by this is the courage to restrain your own potentially destructive impulses. Your anxiety should never affect your workers. Instead, encourage them. Take the heat off of your individual workers and coworkers by pushing everyone, including yourself, as part of a team. The most effective way to lead—and the way that Millennials are predisposed to behave—is to put everyone in the same boat. If we fail, we're all in trouble. If we succeed, we all share pride in the result.

I was once asked to work with an older manager, a man in his mid-50s who had devoted his career to the aerospace business. He had about 110 people—mostly young adults—reporting to him in a machine factory. He was a tough guy, and in his eyes these young workers had no work discipline. But he was in trouble because he was the target of numerous complaints, especially relating to his tendency to chew people out in public. As with the cable TV engineer, my first task was to gain his trust. He told me: "They all know that if they see me coming, they're in trouble." I immediately told him it ought to be the opposite—they should be happy he's coming. Whether good or bad news, your workers need to know you're trying to help them be successful.

As we evolved deeper into his training, one young employee, when asked to redo a task, harshly criticized this man in front of his team. He calculated that the manager would become angry, which would cause him to get into even more trouble with human resources (HR). But the manager by then had gone through "trigger training"—get a word that reminds you of the past, think of it before speaking and remind yourself what your trigger is. So this time the manager didn't flinch; instead he responded by suggesting that they should both meet with HR. The worker then went further with his insults and basically dug his own grave. Subsequently, the manager was praised for how he handled the attack. And the employee who leveled it really stuck out and lost his coworkers' support—he, and not the manager, was fired.

Why was this older manager formerly such a scary guy to his employees? Was he naturally a bad or ornery person? Not at all—in fact, he was obsessed with safety. After taking the time to really get to know him, it came out that he worked at the company that manufactured an aerospace part responsible for the 1986 *Challenger* explosion. He couldn't bear for a similar accident to happen, and that's why he was relentlessly demanding on his factory floor workers. He knew there could be serious consequences if something was not done correctly by his team. He simply needed to learn new leadership skills to ensure that that he could communicate to his team how critical it was for them to pay attention and do things correctly. He was determined that on his watch an accident would never happen like that again.

The approach to problem solving has to change from blame to solution. If someone working is making mistakes, first ask why? Don't just chase what's on the surface—rather, always go to the root cause first. A lot of productivity issues result from a worker's lack of knowledge or training.

A worker can't let on because people will think they're incompetent and they'll get into trouble or possibly be fired. But if you've built trust with your respective workers, then they'll feel free to admit when they're stuck.

Second, reassure them that you've been through this before yourself. You may have never done the exact thing they're doing but think of similar circumstances. Make them feel secure in your understanding and experience of what it feels like to be in their shoes.

And *third*, tell them you'll solve it together. With this approach, you get them over the problem, you've taught them something and can then determine if they're truly capable or not of handling the respective task. So instead of blaming, shouting, or withholding cooperation, you've imparted knowledge. Now you're actually out of confrontation—when you put the emotions connected to the problem off to the side you're fighting together to solve it. It takes the personal out of it, imbues the worker with self-respect, and sets aside the conflict. When your 360—your full coworker and worker— review comes up, you'll receive improved reviews. More importantly, when you need your people to work harder, or when they hit future obstacles and they can't get something done—which they will—you've already set a foundation upon which open communication and cooperation is established.

You've made it so that they won't hesitate to come to you. You've created a safe environment for people to both produce and learn on the job.

Again, here's the formula:

1. First, ask your respective worker or coworkers how they're doing. If they're upset about something, acknowledge that. Identify with the fact that you empathize with them, and make sure they understand that you want to help them. If they say they're fine but you know that to not be true, then affirmatively raise the concern. Until you do this, until things are out in the open, you won't be able to effectively tackle the problem.
2. Identify the problem clearly and objectify it. Look at the problem as if you're standing next to them and examining the problem together; instead of being confrontational, be helpful and *lead them* toward a solution.
3. Tell them you want to help, that you've been through it before. Suggest that you'll solve it together—always first ask their opinion for a solution, even if you already know the solution. Teach them, and take them through the process of solving the problem. If you don't engage people in this way, they'll tend to clam up; you'll never get to the heart of the difficulty or productivity issue, and probably never reach a long-term solution to the problem.

Performance suffers when workers talk behind your back, and you fail to perceive the root causes of any respective problem. On the other hand, challenges are met when an environment of respect and consideration is nurtured. This formula works for everyone—it's part of your leadership kit. This is how human beings operate.

Once I was brought in to consult with a very promising mid-level engineer at a major television network. But the people who worked for him were resigning in droves. All I was told about him was that he was from Asia, and that he was brilliant. At first he was wary of me, feeling defensive—the mere fact that I was asked to speak with him suggested that he was in trouble with the company and that, at the very least, a promotion he was expecting was in jeopardy. He was hurt and upset, and he didn't trust me at all! So I started with the idea that I just wanted to make a new friend—I asked him where he was from. He told me Cambodia. We talked about that for a while, and it turned out that he had escaped the Khmer Rouge as a kid, hiding in trees at night while knowing that he and his family would surely be dead if they were caught. Eventually they made their way to what at the time was South Vietnam, where he managed to attend high school. When the United States pulled out in 1975, and the communist North Vietnamese assumed control, he was put into a prison camp for an extended period. Somehow he managed to be released, and ultimately he made his way to Los Angeles.

This was incredibly important information—considering his background would tell me what motivated his current behavior. He matured in a harsh environment in which everything was literally life or death. So naturally he couldn't relate at all to people who did not approach work with the same life or death attitude—he drove himself so hard, and expected the same from others, because that's what always had worked for him. But none of his coworkers knew about his personal history and the intense environment he came from. Coupled with the fact that he didn't quite grasp American culture, this particular manager was very much in what seemed to be an intractable workplace bind. Once we communicated and learned to trust each other, we went through a number of leadership lessons—how to lead meetings, how to not succumb to emotional triggers. I even had him read U.S. newspapers and business magazines to start to get a feel for American business culture. Ultimately, he was the only engineer in his department to get a promotion. And over the years he's gained even more responsibility, to the point that he now has more than 60 people working for him in two countries.

Generally, each of our days is dominated by three activities: sleeping, working, and spending time with family and loved ones (personal time). Life is relatively short, and we're in bed through a lot of it, so you had better enjoy your working and personal hours. If you, or the people working under you, are neither nourished at the job nor given a path forward—if they're not inspired or encouraged—then performance will undoubtedly suffer.

Why should you care to be a leader rather than merely a manager? Because, for one thing, people will pay a lot of money for a great leader as opposed to a great manager. Great leaders make decisions, they can be direct without offending people, and they will take responsibility off the shoulders of the people to whom they report. Perhaps even more importantly, becoming a leader allows a person to live and interact with others with confidence and courage. Quite apart from earnings, it's confidence and courage that makes a person happy. And whether or not money buys happiness, happy people, at least according to one study, make more money.[1]

For the most part, leaders are capable of making sound decisions based on knowing the true capabilities of the people who work for them. They can be direct because they've gained trust, and everyone knows they'll do their best to make sure each person will succeed. Their bosses see them as supporters and people who take the initiative to solve problems and develop the business—as opposed to being complainers. The people at the top hate complainers. People who complain become nothing but a burden over time and a drain. As soon as the opportunity to replace a complainer comes along, bosses will take it. You're there to help, not gripe about it.

Let's put percentages to it. A 2013 survey found that approximately half of all employees think that workplace morale is decreased in the presence of a toxic coworker; 27 percent were certain that productivity decreases as well. And a whopping 78 percent of workers found coworker negativity to be "extremely debilitating" to team morale and their own individual performance. The fact is that the impact of toxic managers is even greater. If people are unhappy, employees will often spend a good part of their day looking for a new job on the boss's dime. But they're still being paid 100 percent of their salary! That alone is a big hit to productivity and a huge cost.

The demanding, stereotypical, George Steinbrenner–like boss is a management anachronism—especially from the perspective of today's Millennial-generation workers, who expect to be treated with respect. This type of bellicose behavior stems from an old-fashioned notion that you can't be soft in business. Studies have distinguished such toxic managers by four categories: narcissistic, aggressive, rigid, and impaired. Underlying all this, of course, are negative personality traits, including mood disorders and profound insecurities. Basically, these appear to be people with reinforcing destructive patterns by which they unrealistically, and negatively, perceive and interpret the world around them.

But these people can change, because today neither corporations nor even most societies, for that matter, consider bullying to be strength. Self-control is. If toxic management ever worked, it certainly no longer does. It might have had temporary effects, but the best you could achieve through this approach are short-term gains. Running through a number of fired, disgruntled employees is very expensive in the long run, as can be determined by return on investment.[2] Ultimately, it's preferable to establish an environment of trust in which people self-manage; that's when you'll see productivity rates shoot up.

So if toxicity doesn't work, a second approach that many managers try is to tell people, insincerely, that everything will be okay when the manager knows it won't be. This, of course, is a recipe for future disaster, not to mention a rather cowardly way to manage a team. The truth is that a sense of sincerity is the one thing that somehow, in a very subtle way, gets across to others. Human beings perhaps possess some deep inner power that allows them to perceive sincerity instinctively. In fact, in a management setting, sincerity is the key to transforming distrust into trust and hostility into understanding. Trust can't be cultivated strategically. Genuine sincerity opens people's hearts, while manipulation causes them to close. A manipulative approach, at best, complicates the problems and challenges by delaying them for another time. Tackling problems head on shows employees that you care. Even if it's bad news, you're showing you respect them by letting them know what is going on. Delay is the worst thing you can do.

So if shouting doesn't work, and insincerity is no more than a short-term "band-aid" solution, a third way is required to break through. And that third way is to be up front and sincere. I don't mean that you should always reveal everything and be completely transparent. Leadership also has the burden of carrying bad news and stress on your own shoulders and not sharing it—the tension of opposites. Instead, suggest to the people around you that you can't guarantee anything, but let's do our best. Try to get the most out of your group as a whole. Make sure everyone contributes. You do this by creating a culture where everyone is comfortable speaking and every worker is engaged.

Leaders who embrace this approach achieve high rates of productivity—unsatisfied workers may still look for a new job, but they'll also work hard. Their own self-respect is now tied to their performance. Just think of what this saves in turnover costs alone—an unhappy employee is only working part of the time and typically not at their full capacity. Moreover, if they leave, there are significant replacement costs, costs for training new employees, and productivity certainly goes down. To replace a worker you have to pay a recruiter. You have to interview people. You really don't know how a new hire is going to perform until he or she has been on the job for a while. Other coworkers are nervous about new people. A considerable percentage of replacement hires don't work out—as many as 46 percent either resign or are fired within 18 months, according to Leadership IQ.

In fact, 30 case studies taken from the 11 most-relevant research papers on the costs of employee turnover demonstrate that it costs businesses on average about one-fifth of a worker's salary to replace that worker.

One study from the Society for Human Resources Management (SHRM) even found that a replacement could cost up to *five times* a bad hire's annual salary! And the higher the person's position, and the longer they remain in that position, the more it costs in relative dollars to replace him or her.

The bottom line of nurturing empathy and sincerity in dealing with coworkers is that everything is tied to productivity and earnings.

Let's be honest—most people are scared to be personal and open, or to listen to others. But you don't have to be an expert to be a good leader. Nor do you require a position of authority where you work. In fact, anyone can be a good leader.

An excellent example of good leadership is a woman I once worked with named Julie. She's a design engineer and initially worked at a major car company in their racing division. Julie was a quiet and shy person at heart. At the same time, she was a very good engineer and wanted to advance in her career. But she felt repressed and misunderstood, and she didn't like the old-boys club in the department where she was employed. She was teamed with a lot of senior racing veterans, and they resisted the application of new technologies, which was Julie's expertise. Still, Julie also knew that even though they didn't have a good grasp of new technology they had years of actual racing experience that she didn't have—and this intimidated her.

Julie came to me for coaching. My immediate goal was to teach her to lead these guys in a way that would make them feel secure in learning how to use the technology. Basically she had to reach out to them (which was very challenging for her), tell them how much she valued their contributions at work, and get them to trust her. She did exactly that, and ultimately they all appreciated her acknowledgment of their work. When one of them freaked out about having to use a new CAD system (computer design software), she calmed him down and took him to someone in their software department so he could teach this fellow how it worked. They ended up having a great time doing it, and in turn the senior worker thanked Julie profusely for helping him. Julie won these guys over in two weeks. They not only trusted her but also gave her all the support she needed from them to make her department a success.

Yet Julie still wanted to move on and landed a new job at a well-established and successful aerospace company. She immediately invited each one of her coworkers to lunch individually and got to know them personally. She asked each what they felt about their workplace, and with this information she developed suggestions about how to improve some of the company's processes. Because she had invested the time in building relationships with the people she worked with, her colleagues supported her new ideas. Most importantly, the head of engineering for the company reported to Julie's new boss that she was "definitely going places" at the company. Julie accomplished all of this within three weeks' time at a brand new job. That's real leadership.

You simply have to develop compassion and consideration. You have to uncover an ability to teach. These types of managers are hardly soft—because they exercise control over themselves and have a high EQ, they're strong. If you don't develop relationships with your peers and workers, it's going to be very difficult to advance or maintain a successful team. That will take you longer to get to where you want to go. As a result, you'll want to leave for another company. But try to avoid jumping jobs because of all the adjustments that need to be made—and the risk. That's a waste. Instead, spend your time doing what you do well where you are. That's where you will grow.

Ethos, pathos, and logos are the methods to enable workers to overcome their fears and increase productivity and performance, while creating environments that encourage people to want to work. As first set forth by Aristotle more than 2,000 years ago, *ethos* is the ability to project an impression that you're someone worth listening to, as well as someone who is likable and worthy of respect. *Pathos* means persuading by appealing to the listener's emotions. Language choice affects the listener's emotional response, and emotional appeal can effectively be used to enhance an argument. And *logos* means persuading by reason.

So how do we go about combining leadership and management skills with interpersonal development? For that matter, what is leadership in a business context? For one, leaders need to work harder than anyone else and keep striving to develop themselves. People who work hard themselves can appreciate the efforts and challenges of others and offer meaningful support.

Further, a leader doesn't direct anger toward his or her workers or coworkers. Think of being a leader like being a parent. There's a difference between an angry, emotional attack and correcting someone. The way a true leader corrects someone's behavior is with a spirit of encouragement, like the way a mother scolds her child out of love and concern for the child's welfare, or the way a teacher takes a student to task so as to spur the student on to further growth and efforts. Such a leader compassionately points out a person's error. This is truly humanistic encouragement and reflects a spirit of warm and heartfelt concern. Anger, on the other hand, is laced with hate and resentment. Breaking into angry, emotional outbursts is the dark, malicious nature of bullies. Narrow and intolerant people who go around berating others for the slightest thing, or who make a great commotion each time some problem arises, just exhaust everyone and inspire fear. Leaders try to be tolerant and have a warm approachability that makes people feel relaxed and comfortable.

It's been said that in a buffalo herd, all the individuals in the group follow the lead buffalo; they go where he wants to go and they do what he wants to do. In other words, they merely wait for the instructions of the leader. But human organizations don't follow this model—unless they're part of an unthinking herd. Instead, people want to be part of a process, they want to be enfranchised and "own" it—especially Millennials. The ability to nurture this in your colleagues is what makes a good manager a great leader. The mission of a leader is to put everyone's mind at ease, in contrast to the attitude of a boss who tries to manipulate people as if they were machines, assuming that they will do whatever he says. Often they won't, and almost always they'll never do the best they can.

The truth is that piloting your career as a leader, rather than a manager, will not only make you more successful, and increase your company's productivity, but it will also lead you to overcome your fears and be competent and happy yourself. Whether or not you're part of the Millennial generation, the road to confidence in business today is much smoother when you assess how you're feeling, and how others are as well, at any given moment or interaction.

The critical element is to understand that you can do this. So first, before anything else, have hope—like a parent would. The psychologist Martin Seligman, who studies the phenomena of optimism and pessimism, defines optimism as hope. According to him, optimistic people are more likely to succeed at work. That's because they have the conviction that though they might fail they can still take actions to change things.

These skills are even more crucial today as Millennials continue to enter the workforce. The good news is that if you gain their trust and manage them correctly where they feel they should take responsibility within their group, it will spread like a forest fire, because they want to work in groups. They not only want to do it their way, but they also embrace multiple modes of self-expression, demand feedback, and expect empathy and respect in a business setting. If anything, more than any others before, this generation of workers has been better educated and raised with a collaborative ethos. Not only can they easily adapt to the management methods I identify here, but they're already applying them—meaning that everyone else had better catch on fast.

Still, everyone can change, and everyone can learn to be more humanistic and effective. Older people have experience, which the Millennials need; Millennials are valued because they look at things differently, and they are the future of your business or company. Older people can relate on the basis of consideration; the younger ones will follow them if they can make themselves understood within this new and rapidly changing business climate.

NOTES

1. Daniella Miletic, "Money can't buy happiness, but being happy pays," *Sydney Morning Herald* (September 18, 2013), available at http://www.smh.com.au/lifestyle/life/money-cant-buy-happiness-but-being-happy-pays-20130917–2tx7o.html

2. Return on investment is a performance measure used to evaluate the efficiency of an investment or to compare the efficiency of a number of different investments. To calculate ROI, the benefit of an investment is divided by the cost of the investment; the result is expressed as a percentage or a ratio.

Chapter 2

The Privilege of Leadership

The Simultaneity of Cause and Effect

Everything you do matters, and every cause has its effect. Business leaders—Millennial or not—first must consider how they themselves would want to be treated, and then apply that understanding toward more empathetic relationships with their employees. Chances are that most people desire the following:

- Someone who cares about you and your work environment.
- Somebody who listens to you even when you're upset or angry.
- Someone who is loyal to you.
- Someone who acknowledges your work.
- Someone who helps to teach or train you when you need it.
- Someone who doesn't keep you out of the loop and leave you guessing about what's happening with the company.
- Someone who will protect you and stand up for you.

Although considered by some a "soft" approach, humanistic leadership is far from an easy task. In fact, it's a contact sport, you have to be patient and strong. Get a helmet you may need it. A humanistic management vision is grounded in the understanding that people will never forget a supervisor's positive efforts on their behalf. The payback is both increased productivity for the organization and confidence and real competency as a management leader.

So in what sort of soil is such an approach rooted? For me, it's a combination of Buddhist philosophy and real-world business experience. Many years ago I was attracted to and began to study Buddhism. I think the emphasis in this philosophy on compassion and personal liberty was what most appealed to me. I suppose I was somewhat of an idealist, and I wanted to do the right thing by others.

Back when I was younger, though, the business world had me stumped. I grew up as a shy, kind of quiet kid. Coming from a family of musicians, I was creative by nature, and I suppose I had developed certain sensitivities to art and culture. Perhaps this was, in part, why I was always bothered by the dichotomy between being a caring person and the reality, as I perceived it, of how people actually acted in business. It's not so much that I couldn't handle hard-driving, single-minded individuals; in fact, I knew all about people who were both highly talented and emotional. Balancing such personal dichotomies was second nature to me.

In time, it was through my experience and my practice of Buddhism that I learned the most about people, what makes them happy and unhappy, and what gets them to strive to do good work and reach their true potential. This book is based on the desire for people to become happy and productive at the same time in a highly competitive world. The book is for today's leaders and managers who are trying to succeed in a rapidly changing economy while creating profitable and companies where people can happily thrive. It's also about the future generation of leaders coming into the workforce now and beginning to shape the work environment differently, in ways few members of an established generation of leaders can understand. At the end of the day, our objectives must be to create a working environment that's highly successful and profitable, while being one where everyone is treated with dignity and respect, and in turn treats others the same.

But back when I started my career I suppose I just wasn't smart enough to figure out how to do both things well—care about people while also seizing the advantage in business. Just before graduating from college I secured a terrific job on a national network weekly music show called *The Midnight Special.* I was 23 years old at the time—the same age as today's younger Millennials. I really liked everyone that I worked with, and although I was competitive and wanting to advance, I was just thrilled to have the job and enjoyed every day. After all, I worked with many of the top rock and music artists of the time.

Then I was promoted in rapid succession and took on three responsibilities—one was especially critical for the success of the show. It came with an unreal amount of pressure, and although I knew the music business well having grown up in it, nothing—and I mean nothing—prepared me for managing people and politics. I could handle short-term situations, like a two-day production here and there, because nothing lasted long enough for me to run into any real trouble handling crews or talent. But in the greater scheme of things on an ongoing television series, I had no idea how to handle the executives and crew I had to work with.

I was young, and so I felt I had to prove myself, as all young people do when they're challenged and scared. As a result, I became aloof, aggressive, and defensive. I didn't take criticism well at all, and I felt I had to do everything perfectly, so when I naturally made a mistake I took it personally and would get extremely angry with myself—which also meant there was a very good possibility someone around me might catch some of my wrath. This eventually spiraled into deep unhappiness, and I completely lost my love for the job and what I was doing.

And what a shame that was. I remember one day sitting in a meeting with someone who had mentored me and given me a lot of opportunities, saying out loud to me, "What happened to you? You used to be such a great kid, but now you're pissed off all time and taking everything so seriously." In other words, I was a negative drag to be around. This guy was someone I looked up to, and it really hurt when he said it. I was a fairly typical case of someone thrust into a management role with no leadership training whatsoever.

The cost of not knowing how to lead was very high. From that point on it was a struggle, and most of what I ultimately learned came through mentors and self-study in progressively greater and harder leadership roles in different businesses.

But that development took a very long time, and I was never truly confident that I was leading or managing well until after the fact—when someone might say I did a good job. This is a very stressful way to live—not knowing what to do with everyone expecting you to know what to do is a common and an awful position to be in.

So in business, for years, I struggled between balancing my instincts to care for people and the reality of acting aggressively to be successful. And to me, for whatever reason, it felt as if these conditions were inherently and mutually exclusive.

I was not easily intimidated at all, but when it came to business I knew that I knew nothing. Although an MBA isn't particularly necessary, I did recognize my need to understand the fundamentals of business. And slowly it dawned on me that a leader also has to understand human beings as a critical component of doing business—knowing one without the other is lopsided at best. Eventually, I started to connect my Buddhist worldview with what I was experiencing in a tough and highly competitive work environment, eventually an understanding dawned on me of cause and effect.

What I discovered back then was that I couldn't just worry about myself and where I was going—things would be short term and then I'd leave and not be happy. I had to focus on other people—that made me happier, and it made me more successful.

Eventually I got tired of sitting across the table and listening to people argue about deal-making while I had no idea what they were talking about. And I did eventually go back to school to earn an MBA, at Loyola Marymount in Los Angeles, California. And it was right around this time when I started to understand the difference between true leadership and simple management.

By this point I had a basis to blend the personal skills I had developed through Buddhism with the real fundamentals of business—how to get financing, how to set expectations, and so on. I knew now what I had to do, which made it easier to outline for people what they had to do. I started to see how mistakes were made by assuming things, and especially how business leaders had a tough time encouraging people who worked for them. Treating people poorly will eventually bite you.

According to Buddhism, everything is in a constant state of flux. So the question becomes whether to be swept away by changes in business circumstances and environments or rather create positive changes through our own efforts—or, in a surfing context, whether to ride the wave or be engulfed by it. One famous Buddhist sutra goes like this: "If you want to understand the causes that existed in the past, look at the results as they are manifested in the present. And if you want to understand what results will be manifested in the future, look at the causes that exist in the present."

Well, let me tell you, I was very unhappy living as the aggressor at my workplace. People were scared of me. Others were positively out to get me. Those under me, the people I managed, did what I asked them to do out of fear. And in retrospect I can see that I didn't come close to getting the most out of them.

Not that this is an easy thing to do—indeed, how do you do this? Well, it's always the present moment that counts. Don't have regrets about your past. Truly, it doesn't matter in business what you did in the past, because if you bring out your best in the present moment then it's that past that led you to do your best. Similarly, if you're doing your utmost in the present moment you don't need to be anxious about your future. The past doesn't govern our future—the present moment does. No matter what we've done in the past we can still create a more valuable future. This is a critical point that we'll return to throughout this book. Have confidence starting right now that you can do this.

The only way to learn how to succeed in business leadership is to practice doing business. Here's a big secret that business professors won't tell you—you learn very little from theory unless you can apply it to real-life situations. Always seek out actionable information. How do you attack what you're facing this minute? It doesn't matter if you're a business owner, a founder, a manager, or an employee. It doesn't matter if you're a baby boomer, a Millennial, or Generation X. The bottom line is to figure out how to overcome what's in front of your face so you can create a profitable work environment and still sleep soundly at night.

Look at executive education. Most people enrolled in these university-level programs don't have any time to really put into them. So what happens is that you pay a lot of money for subject matter experts in each field to slam down your throat too much information in a matter of a few days. Even the smartest people will only retain part of that. But it sticks when you teach someone how to apply it right away in his or her work environment. They get results, and then they're happy. Actual practice, and not theory, is the only way to become successful with business fundamentals.

After working in entertainment I started gravitating toward new industries with younger people. Often I met, for example, software developers who were incredibly talented but didn't know how to write a letter. The speed of business increases dramatically each year. Companies can get out of control in no time at all. If you don't create the right culture quickly, things will implode. Big Fortune 500 companies can hang on for a while, but that's not the majority of businesses in the United States.

Mentoring is critical in business. A mentor, of course, is someone who guides a less experienced person by, for example, building trust or modeling positive behaviors. You might feel you're doing just fine by yourself, but for most people the truth is that eventually someone without a mentor will become self-centered, capricious, and arrogant—exactly the attributes a leader should try to avoid. Don't confuse a mentor with a master—a master might enslave someone, but a mentor builds bridges for the less experienced person to walk across.

Try to recall a boss who guided and helped you. Write down what they did for you, and then write down how that made you feel. Finally, write down the effect and results it had on your career.

Now pick some employees who *need* your help. Write down their job description, what's expected of them—do a SWOT analysis on them. Evaluate their Strengths, Weaknesses, Opportunities, and Threats.

Now determine what they need to learn, how long they have to learn it, and what exactly you will teach/mentor them. Lastly, determine how and when you will help them. Be specific so you know you can hold up your end of the bargain, and they will know what is expected of them.

The payback is both increased productivity for the organization and confidence and real competency as a management leader.

How does mentoring increase productivity? For one, you'll no longer waste hours, days, weeks, or months being frustrated with somebody who isn't getting the job done. I've found that more often than not the reason for poor performance isn't a poor attitude or lack of ability, it's lack of knowledge or experience. When someone gets a job or a promotion, it's usually assumed that he or she knows how to do the job. What we fail to acknowledge much of the time is that he or she may know 70, or 80, or even 95 percent of the job, but not all of it—and that remaining 5 percent can make the difference between success or failure. By developing humanistic leadership skills you form a relationship with workers based on trust, not one based on being frustrated, critical or judgmental, which of course causes the person to become defensive and operate from a place of fear. Then you're screwed as a manager. You may never figure out exactly what the problem was with the worker, or what knowledge he or she was missing. Simultaneously you've destroyed the possibility of the worker's improving, and you've potentially lost a valuable employee. *You* are the only one who can fix all of this by developing a proactive and helpful attitude toward the employee.

People of Millennial-generation age not only expect to be nurtured and mentored in business but often seek it out. Workers aged 20–35 are already predisposed to not wanting to be shouted at, for example, but instead related to with consideration and respect. Millennials, in general, won't put up with being disrespected—this is sometimes incorrectly perceived as being soft or weak. In a certain sense, an outlook like this is courageous, even if many don't understand the potential consequences of such an attitude in the workplace.

I once worked with a group of designers responsible for an expensive and critical engineering prototype that was being tested for reliability. They were all Millennial-age and very smart and well educated, with an abundance of confidence. Just as they were about to conduct the test a more senior designer caught a huge mistake, a miscalculation that would have caused the entire test and the prototype to fail. One member of the design team was responsible for this mistake. This caused the entire team to look bad, and they deservedly caught hell for it. Obviously, the team was very unhappy with the guy who screwed up, which was a boneheaded one that could have been avoided. I had actually coached this individual for a couple of sessions, and I knew he generally was afraid, insecure, and defensive. This nature prompted him to not seek advice or get his work checked before the event. His insecurity manifested as arrogance, and he had been repelling a lot of his team members.

Then something interesting happened.

The senior designer jumped on this guy when he found out it was his mistake. He slipped up by attacking him personally, calling him lazy. What happened next was astounding. His entire team jumped to his defense, all at once. They called the senior designer an asshole, and who was he to treat a member of their team that way? Literally, they all lined up against the senior designer and complained to human resources.

The moral here is to refrain from insulting people. Millennials have already learned something at a young age that some of us never learn—do not disrespect people. You may criticize their performance, but it better be based on logic, reason, and facts. This senior guy got his butt kicked by HR and, moreover, was sent to me for personal coaching.

Humanistic leadership also saves time and money and increases productivity. Why would you invest in people, teach them how the company works, train them until they understand their job—and now simply fire them. Do you really want to start all over again? You have no idea if a new person will be successful. And what if they don't get along with people already working there? Have you nurtured the rest of your team to the extent that they can even accept new people? Isn't it easier to turn around that one person instead? Firing someone brings out the worst in everyone. But you need skills to break through these problems fast—at the end of the day if things don't work out make damn sure that it's a business decision and not based on a clash of personalities. Try not to run your human resources based on a gauge of interpersonal weaknesses.

I recall coaching a shop foreman who was one of the best machinists a particular company had. He knew the job inside out, and his bosses (a director and a VP above the director) completely depended on him, especially in a time of crisis. Unfortunately he had a reputation for being impatient and overly critical of people who worked for him.

By the time I started with him it had reached the point that he and one of his workers would regularly shout at each other. This of course happened on the shop floor, making everyone else uptight and demoralizing the entire team. HR was really in a quandary—they needed this guy, but they couldn't allow the way he managed people to continue.

He was 64 years old, from a foreign country, and had experienced firsthand as a private citizen a terrible war. He was angry about needing the coaching; he thought he was in the right and that he was not appreciated or listened to by the company. So I let him vent and then asked him about his background. Of course he had been trained in an incredibly strict environment where any mistake or complaint resulted in immediate firing, or worse. We discussed the difference between the United States and his birth country, and I slowly gained his trust. At that point I took him through basic leadership skills, how to solve problems, how to show someone compassion and diffuse a problem. Then I showed him how to instill a sense of pride in the people that worked for him.

There was one guy in particular who constantly complained and drove my client crazy—his name was Benjamin. Benjamin was a good machinist, but constantly griped about his position, his hours, vacation time, and why he hadn't been promoted to a Lead yet. By this time my client would simply avoid him, so there would be no opportunity for any communications whatsoever.

Benjamin, though, was starting to make mistakes and negatively influencing the younger workers on the team. They were slowing down and not seeking training. This resulted in more scrapped parts, delayed deliveries, and extra hours to build new parts that would work. My client had yelled at them so many times that they no longer heard him. They *expected* to get yelled at, so they just looked at it as part of the job.

This was the perfect setup to get things turned around.

I told my client that he had to get over his anger toward Benjamin, and that he should actually have Benjamin lead the turnaround. Needless to say he was shocked. In fact, he said I was nuts. But I perceived the primary reason that Benjamin was complaining so much was that no one was paying attention to him. He's just like the rest of us—he needs to be acknowledged for his effort and contribution. I asked my client to re-instill pride in Benjamin, show him how important he was to the company, and, most importantly, how much my client depended on him. Again shock, as expected—my guy had never even considered such an approach.

But I told him how to do it. He needed to sit down with Benjamin away from the job site, at lunch or over a beer, and literally tell him that he wouldn't know what he would do without him. And that he depended on him to lead the team, even though he didn't have the Lead title yet. And that he was the one that the younger workers would look up to and would follow. My client *needed* him to do that, or the entire team would fail.

The next day Benjamin started turning things around. He began training two of the younger workers so they would stop making mistakes. He then organized team meetings to go over how productive they had been each week and where they needed to improve. Naturally, the mistakes decreased in just two weeks. Overtime was reduced, because parts weren't being remade. Scrapped parts went down so material costs were reduced. At that point the team was given more parts to build because of their increased efficiency and productivity. My client calmed down a lot, the yelling stopped, and he made sure he met with Benjamin at least twice a week to determine whether he was okay and to thank him for what he had accomplished.

Why would Benjamin do all of this without getting a raise or the Lead promotion? He did it because he felt responsible for his team's success, and he understood he was appreciated and acknowledged for his hard work. This is a small example of the increased productivity that humanistic leadership can produce. To this day Benjamin's great work continues, and he was promoted to Lead for his efforts. My client, in turn, is managing more people now and raising capable people under him to become Leads in the future.

Again, if you want to change the future look at the causes you're making in the present. Millennials seem to inherently grasp this point. Against all odds, they're optimistic about the future. Do these people live in the same community as the rest of the world? For the most part, yes—it's those of the older population who are outside of it.

Think about it—Millennials "hang out" in virtual communities. They were born into the electronic revolution that most of the rest of us adapted to. The youngest of them are, at least in America, generally supported financially by their parents, driven to exploit the best educational opportunities and raised to be cynical by their (often hypocritical) baby boomer parents. And there are a lot of them—24 year olds are the largest age demographic in the United States.

Millennials, of course, don't care about the corporation like older workers once did. They say they're in it for the social values that a job might engender, but in truth most of them are in it for themselves. There's virtually no loyalty to a company, so you had better provide for them a real career path. Nothing scares a Millennial more than to tell them they're set at the company for the rest of their lives. They'll run screaming from the room. They see themselves as mobile, socially conscious, and intrepid. If you have very good employees of this generation you had better think about how to best nurture them, according to the mentoring models already discussed. Loyalty is a relative term for them. At the same time sincerity is an attribute they, as all others, will respect.

To dip into some shallow Buddhist waters, again, we might consider a concept known as dependent origination. This concept expresses a truth that everything in the universe, including everyone's life, is interconnected. Nothing exists in isolation. In fact, all beings and phenomena exist only because of their relationship with other beings or phenomena. The Buddha once used the image of two bundles of reeds to demonstrate this principle. Each can remain standing as long as both lean against one another.

An awareness of such interconnectedness is critical to becoming a successful business leader in today's environment.

Chapter 3

Getting Out of Your Own Way

Emotional Triggers and Building a Solid Self

The only thing of real value that a manager has is the ability to change himself or herself. But the only way we can actually change and ultimately improve productivity is to first become aware of what about ourselves most needs to be changed or better managed—our emotional triggers. Only then can we develop an ability to recognize the emotional triggers in others with whom we work.

Emotional triggers are events or occurrences that elicit deeply ingrained responses that often have little to do with the event or occurrence at hand. These are very personal psychological response mechanisms, and the same event will trigger different things in different people. In business, a person's triggers most often are activated by what someone else says or does. Occasionally we may even respond to how another person simply looks or even smells.

Such triggers aren't inherently negative—rather, the defense mechanism to an earlier trauma is developed within each of us to protect ourselves. But often we see people overreacting to some conflict at work. In these cases, a person's emotional trigger is forcefully resulting in a response that to others appears as if it has nothing to do with the situation at hand. Such out-of-proportion reactions cause big problems at work—if someone's been conditioned to respond to a trigger caused by, for example, a real childhood trauma, then he or she poses a potential management issue if the business leader (1) is unaware of what's actually going on and (2) fails to diffuse it.

Our defense mechanisms are typically triggered when we feel someone isn't honoring our own self-image or the qualities that we think make us special. What is it that sets off our own emotional triggers, what causes us to feel personally wounded in the most intimate of ways? Take a look at the following list and see if you can identify which attacks most set you off:

- Feeling unaccepted or rejected
- Impugned integrity, or questions about honesty
- General disapproval
- Threats to control
- Unavailability of someone necessary
- Doubts about respect
- Being blamed or unfairly judged
- Perceived unfair treatment
- Whether or not you're liked
- Whether you're understood
- Whether you're needed
- Not feeling valued
- A need to be right
- Questions about attentiveness or interest
- Doubts about intelligence
- Questions about safety
- Acceptance of new challenges
- Threats to autonomy

Which of these needs are most important to you? And which, when triggered, make you feel most threatened?

The problem, of course, is that as we make our way through life, our brains become accustomed to a keen awareness for situations that may threaten our most intimate needs in even the slightest of ways. And without any conscious thought, we all in a sense become enslaved to these emotions and find ourselves often reacting involuntarily, instinctively, and without thinking when some deep wound is triggered—inadvertently or not. When our responses fail to be in proportion to the triggering event, we tend to inject negativity into the workplace environment.

So take a look at the previous list and try to identify your primary triggers. Next, consider when and where such behavior typically occurs. And third, think real hard about what you accomplish by reacting in the ways you typically do.

As an exercise, get a blank paper or pull up a document and describe what's generally a high-risk emotional trigger for you. Identify a time when something like this actually occurred, and then describe it in detail. Include what happened, why it happened, and especially how you reacted.

Next, list all of the consequences of how you behaved in response to the triggering event. List both the positive and negative effects of your behavior and note whether these reactions happened instantly, or some time later.

It's completely normal to be wound up about something—so identify what it is that sets you off. What causes it? Recognize that it's not actually about the person you're dealing with but is instead anchored in something inside of you. If the trigger tends to initiate a cascade of negative results, then the idea is to learn how not to react the same way anymore. Managers are in leadership positions because someone believes in them. They want it to work. If you're handcuffed by your own emotional triggers—circumstances that cause you to be angry, for example—remember that the people you're dealing with have no idea what those issues are and what's running through your brain.

The key training for leaders is to get control of themselves. Rise above any situation. Create your own culture; the culture of the company or organization is irrelevant in most cases. By investing in yourself, giving yourself a break, figuring out your triggers and what makes you weak instead of strong, you'll turn negative tendencies into strengths and advance your department's productivity. A solid self is built one step at a time, and it is very hard to topple.

So as challenging as it might be to gain control over ourselves, it's actually impossible to do so over others. But you don't have to—instead you have to learn how to recognize what it is that sets people off on their own emotional trigger responses. Study your workers, coworkers, and supervisors, of whatever age; really get to know them; and understand why they behave the ways that they do.

You can't necessarily understand completely what other people are going through—and sometimes even they don't either. But wouldn't you have so much more of an upper hand if you find out as much as you can about them before you react or overreact? Otherwise, if you just try to be tough, you'll toughen people right up and out of your company. Millennials, in particular, generally cast a wary eye on human nature and have no intrinsic loyalty to a company or a firm. Anyone can get angry and blow it—that doesn't make you tough, and Millennials often perceive that as weak. Being really tough is the ability to handle oneself—to do the best you can without dumping on everyone else, no matter the circumstances.

It's the art of maintaining, as Morrie Schwartz famously said, "the tension of opposites."

People react a certain way. I let them react and then ask what's upsetting them. Let them complain about their boss or employee. After they finish I say, first, you're doing that isn't going to change anything at all. In fact, you're exacerbating a problem and making it worse. There's nothing wrong with righteous or justified anger, but you can't let it control you. Does your anger create any value at all? That's the first place to start. If you think you feel better about releasing it, what's actually happening is that you're dispensing negative energy. Acting from a place of anger is like drinking poison and expecting the other person to die. Once you do that you've lost control and given up all power. If you're the boss, and you've lost control through an inability to control your anger, well, let's say it doesn't bode well for your career or for people from whom you require respect. Managing others through fear is one of the stupidest things you can do.

Buddhism teaches that the important thing is to firmly fix our gaze on our own weaknesses—not run away from them, but to battle them head-on and establish a solid self that nothing can sway. Interoffice hardships, therefore, forge and polish our lives, so that eventually they make us stronger and better leaders, leading, of course, to increased profitability. The truth is that people rooted in the here and now, people not defeated by their limitations or intimidated by others—people who don't compare themselves to others—can confidently advance both in business and in life in general.

There is a lot at stake if you fail to learn how to control yourself.

I once worked with a young guy, a supremely talented Millennial worker named Peter—he had a massive business responsibility leading a variety of people in an intense corporate environment. Peter was the type of guy to get down in the trenches with a do-it-yourself attitude. But he was killing himself, and no one under him was growing.

For Peter, the emotional trigger was insecurity—he had been burned in the past by people saying they'd do something but then fail to come through. As a result, he would defer to panic and micro-management rather than delegating responsibility. The belief that you need to do everything yourself is a common emotional trigger that actually will destroy you at work. And it's a trait that I've seen over and over again, particularly in Millennial-generation workers.

In my coaching I've found that there are two subcategories related to Peter's particular trigger. One is the belief some have that if they don't do it, it won't be done right (this has the dual aspect of arrogance and insecurity). Second is the feeling that if others are allowed to complete certain assignments, then the supervisor may no longer have the same value or worth to the company as they once did (job security).

Peter was an accomplished engineer. He was so capable and knowledgeable that he was put in charge of four different and critical teams at his company. All four of these teams had high-profile projects they were responsible for, and if any of them failed it would literally be catastrophic for the business. Peter knew this well because of his past experience, and he had a good idea of the level of detail that had to be adhered to for these projects to be successful. That was both good news and bad news.

Peter, like most engineers, had very little management training despite having earned graduate-level degrees from both Stanford and MIT. When I first met him, I saw what a likeable and capable guy he was. I also saw the red circles under his eyes and stress in his face. Here was a guy who was physically fit but looked much older than he was from all of the pressure that he was under.

I asked him why he was so stressed, and he listed all of the meetings he had to attend and still make all of the deadlines for his different projects. He couldn't be in two places at once, so a lot of work had to wait until he could be there to oversee it. Here was an incredibly smart guy, and yet he was just beginning to figure out that it all wasn't going to get done this way! I then told him that there was also no way that he himself would survive managing the way he did. He was definitely going to burn out, and he agreed it wouldn't take long at the rate he was going.

The next question I asked was how good the people were who worked for him in these four teams. He said they were all terrific, intelligent, and hard working. So why didn't he let them do the work themselves, and come to him when they only needed help?

"What if they screw it up?" he asked. "They haven't done this all the way through before." Then why were they hired? His response was because they were so good at what they did. So his logical mind knew they could do the work, but his emotional trigger was screaming NO WAY!

I could see the quandary he was in, and he admitted it. It wasn't rational. It was because he was afraid they wouldn't do it. As good and responsible as they had proven to be, he still was nervous about letting go of the controls. If he let that emotional response control his management style, then these individuals would never grow to handle the teams themselves—and he would literally handcuff his own career. He, himself, would also fail to grow or take on more responsibilities.

We went through his past work experiences, and he talked about times when the people he was working with had betrayed him by saying they were getting something done, and then they didn't deliver. He ended up getting pounded by the CEO of one company for not delivering a project on time. In fact, this happened to him more than once, and being a perfectionist he then started micromanaging every aspect of the projects at his previous job. This led to resentment from the rest of his team. It also led to a deepening of mistrust. He didn't count on them to get things done on their own, and they didn't trust him in return. We came up with a word that would remind him of that time, and that when he started feeling the urge to "jump in" and run things he would think of the word and stop before he did.

Of course, more than a simple word was required—he also had to learn to control the underlying triggering emotion, and he needed to create system or plan that would allow him to feel secure that the teams were going to deliver.

We then went through the teams and team leaders. We quickly identified one or two people on each team that with just a little more training and support were very capable of leading others and getting the projects done. Peter was all for it—he was elated at the thought of catching a break and maybe even taking a day off. He met with them individually, and they mutually came up with a check-in procedure that would both keep Peter in the loop and enable them to ask for help when they needed it. He subsequently met with the teams and empowered the team leaders in front of everyone to manage the projects without his involvement.

Since that time Peter has been assigned another team under his command, and two of his team leaders have been promoted to managers. Peter even took a vacation of four days—in his world that's equivalent to three weeks! He's conspicuously less stressed, and now looks at what emotional trigger may be influencing him when he starts to feel stressed and wants to "get back into the trenches." And he didn't change overnight—it took Peter three months for him to really stay out of the day-to-day battles. But he got there, and his career and the careers of some of his reports have grown as well.

Life is not going to necessarily turn out as we hope or plan. The important thing is to fix our gaze on our own weaknesses. Don't run away from them. Rather, battle them head-on and establish a solid self that nothing and no one can sway. Difficulties are opportunities to improve and become stronger. That's why it's critical to become the master of one's mind, rather than being mastered by it.

So if the first step is to gain control over our personal triggers, the second is to step into your coworker's shoes. How would you react, honestly, if someone were to speak to you in an abrupt and dismissive manner? Probably you'd want to knock their teeth in. At the very least, you'd be upset and not inclined to want to talk to them ever again.

Let's look at this from the standpoint of what's really upsetting. Leaving psychology to the psychologists, it's just a fact that what triggers our emotional responses are things we're upset about from long ago and far away.

When our emotions are triggered, we tend to be defensive or covering up as a response to something shoved into our heads from another time. For all the different techniques and interpersonal skills that we might be exposed to, if I throw you up against a wall you're going to react like you would have when you were 12 years old. At least that's normally what happens.

How does one master such a base, instinctual, and seemingly natural angry response? Here's how: by grabbing your emotional trigger before you react. Get control first *before* you respond.

Think of a word that reminds you of the past. A lot of tech and computer engineers think of the word "legacy," as in a legacy software system. Write it down. Put it on a pad before you speak to anyone. Associate that word with the old way of doing things. And before you open your mouth think of the word—then speak. Give yourself a break, a pause, to consider and possibly rethink what you're going to say.

How do we know when the emotional trigger has been stimulated? Well, as soon as you start to feel the anger bubbling up—capture it. What's really bothering you? What does it remind you of? Most people can catch it. When the feeling comes up, first identify the deeper cause before falling out of control. Then set aside the anger and deal with your problem rationally. Put it where it belongs—not in your mouth or your head. It's a karmic journey that's very hard to return from—once you're worked up it's very hard to stop. You'll keep going down that circular path of anger, followed by defense, leading to suppressed rage, and then back to anger again.

When a bruised emotional trigger leads to the acting out of anger, as it typically does, then the damage goes way beyond the person you're dealing with. In most social situations, and especially in workplaces, the first thing people talk about is bad news. Anger infects your entire business community. If you express it in front of others, it's even worse. Now everyone's heard it, they'll all have an opinion on it, and probably they'll be more fearful than the person you're chewing out. I think often in this regard of the scenes from *Fiddler on the Roof*, and how a letter becomes gossip for the villagers, who turn it into a song that totally distorts the truth. The fact is that the person most damaged by your anger is you.

As many Millennials entering the workplace have discovered, they typically will be assigned to departments headed by older men or women. Steven was one such middle-aged middle manager who supervised production lines. He had more than 30 years of experience, and not only knew how to manage a production line, but he also knew all of the special equipment that was needed to produce the parts and all of the manufacturers who made them. He would participate in the annual negotiations for buying new equipment, which cost tens of millions of dollars. This made him very valuable to his company.

But Steven had not been promoted past the director level for more than 10 years. He made a comfortable living—and also had a couple of expensive hobbies outside of work that took up most of his free time. Steven was a very sharp guy, and he certainly had the brainpower to become a vice president if he wanted to. What Steven lacked, however, was the ability to correct his staff without insulting them. He was impatient, and he was angry. He couldn't understand why people didn't get things as quickly as he did. He would explain something once, and if someone asked a question his response was usually, "I just told you how to do it!" So people were afraid to ask him a question. They would just go on doing things incorrectly until everything came to a grinding halt.

One of the basic aspects of manufacturing parts is that there will be certain amounts of "scrapped parts" that had imperfections in them, or bore mistakes in the manufacturing process and were therefore unusable. Notably, individual workers and teams could be judged based on the amount of scrap they produced. The more scrap the least efficiency—scrap was expensive because of the wasted man-hours, and the wasted materials. And in Steven's business raw materials were very expensive.

Eventually the amount of scrap his department produced climbed to an alarming rate. On top of that, many of his workers had complained to HR about Steven's management style—or lack thereof. Some of his reports had been on the job for more than five years, they took a great deal of pride in their work, and they were sick and tired of being treated as if they were stupid. I was asked to coach Steven. As valuable as he was, he also created a horrible culture in his department. The poor quality of the work was slowing things down and costing the company money.

The first thing I noticed was Steven's temper. When he talked about certain members of his team, he would get red faced and angry. They were making him look bad, even after "I told them exactly how to do things correctly. Why the hell didn't they get it?"

He knew he was in trouble, which probably added to his anger. He also wanted to get promoted and finish his career as a vice president. And he needed the money that a promotion would bring him. The truth was that at this point the possibility of a promotion was almost gone. His boss needed him, but at the same time he couldn't take the unhappy workers constantly complaining.

So the first thing Steven had to learn was how he blamed everyone else for everything that wasn't working—starting with his boss, who "didn't listen to me, and then didn't include me in every meeting." Then he blamed the veteran workers for the constant mistakes and increasing levels of scrapped parts. Even though, with the new machines they were using, there were things they would have to learn differently. So everyone else but him was to blame? I suggested that that was the core of all of his difficulties.

By constantly looking at his environment as the source of all of his problems he never looked at himself. And that's why he was perpetually angry. The environment would refuse to cooperate with how he thought things should be! I pointed out him that he was responsible for his environment, at least from the standpoint of his attitude. Cause and effect is strict. If you spend a great deal of time being angry, don't expect the world to give you a big hug and tell you that's okay. Your environment will respond in kind.

In Steven's case, the people who worked for him were pissed off at how little he respected them. When they complained about him, it wasn't mildly. The younger Millennial age workers just flat out wouldn't talk to him unless they absolutely had no other choice. They had written him off as a cranky old guy who would never look out for them or help them. Herein lies the lesson: Steven had cut himself off from the veteran workers, whom he needed to lead the teams he was responsible for. At the same time he had alienated himself from the Millennials who, of course, were the future—and more importantly *his* future. There wasn't anyway he'd be promoted without continuing to manage the group he already had.

Steven did the best he could with the coaching, and he used the techniques of problem solving especially with the younger workers. He was able to get much closer to most of them, and they started to appreciate him for his knowledge and his experience. Remember the Millennials *expected* him to help them, they're looking for guidance and support from their leaders. In the end, Steven made it a priority to raise new managers from that age group.

Unfortunately the same didn't hold true for the veteran workers. When someone is at their final position in their career, and they're no longer climbing up the ladder, their entire worth at the company is based on the job they currently have. Hence they take great pride in what they do and naturally are more set in their ways. If you shout at them and don't acknowledge their knowledge and experience you can expect real anger, not cooperation, to come your way. And guess what? You deserve it. They're human beings and their time on this planet is just as valuable as yours or anyone else's. If you fail to learn to treat them with respect, you'll suffer the consequences, as Steven did. Most of them transferred or left the company, and Steven was faced with replacing them—that took a lot of time and cost the company money. This stymied any chance of a promotion for Steven, as he now didn't have the time to take on additional responsibilities because he was compelled to rebuild his department.

Still, Steven was much happier and calmer, and he did learn to take charge of his emotional triggers, manage his anger, and conquer his communication weaknesses at work. He also took pride in raising the next group of managers from his younger group of reports.

Over time, people will learn what their triggers are. It's not something to master right away—rather, it's more like two steps forward, one step back. Just be keen to make progress; it'll take time to get your head around it. Start by writing down that word as your key to reminding you of your past, and start to figure out what to do about it.

Chapter 4

People Are Your Resources

Focus on Others to Get What You Want

A primary objective for leaders should be to find managers who know how to lead other people. If such mid-to-high–level managers are doing their jobs, then the organizational leaders are free to do what they most need to do and concentrate on the big picture. People are your resources, and you need to focus on them in order to be effective. If you constantly worry about your internal standing, then you won't achieve measureable results. And you can make yourself literally sick in the process, miserable, and not wanting to go to work because all you're worried about is politics. You'll never get over yourself. Instead, to be most effective, focus on people in your organization—this is how you become more valuable to the company.

Politics or strong-arming eventually will fail to work, because the higher you rise the more your actual weaknesses will be exposed. When you turn around for support, there will be no one there, and no one will follow you. When you slip and fall, and make mistakes, which you will—if you've been strong-arming you won't have a lifejacket. You'll be exposed, so good luck on your own.

There are lots of examples of these sorts of falls by arrogant individuals who had no one to soften their landings when times got rough. The resignation of New York governor Eliot Spitzer in 2008 is particularly instructive.

Spitzer had been elected governor in 2007, and almost immediately there was speculation that he'd one day be a candidate for president of the United States. Prior to becoming governor, Spitzer was a high-profile state

BAKER COLLEGE of CLINTON IWD LIBRARY

attorney general, and he became famous for his investigations of insurance company frauds, mutual fund trading scandals, and other securities frauds, in addition to many other prosecutions. He was a very popular attorney general, and a media darling—at one point in 2004 a major publication recommended him to be the Democratic Party's vice presidential candidate.

But Spitzer was reportedly very difficult to work for, and with, and he alienated many powerful businesspeople, lawyers, politicians, and reporters during his rise to the governorship. And so in March 2008, when it was reported that he had hired prostitutes, Spitzer's fall was exceedingly swift and lonely. He was compelled to resign only seven days after the initial reports, was never again elected to political office, and ultimately suffered a barrage of vicious public criticism that continues to some extent even until today.

What happened? Surely a politician won't typically survive a revelation of illegal activity, but the dearth of support in any way for an individual that only a few years earlier was the toast of New York was breathtaking. The truth is that he made so many enemies that as soon as his position was threatened, as soon as there was blood in the water, so to speak, the sharks were prepared to tear him apart. The man was at the top of his field, but he had no friends or supporters to catch him when he slipped.

Examine very closely the current status of your company culture. What sort of an environment is created when leaders are brash, self-centered, or even abusive and don't care for helping others? Consider whether any of the following sounds familiar:

- Bad morale
- Backstabbing
- Negative politics
- Outmaneuvering among coworkers
- Silos and turf wars, with department heads not cooperating with other departments, trying to grab other peoples' projects, building walls and barriers
- Hoarding of information, and allowing someone to fail to make others look better than they are
- Lack of unity, where individual goals are more important than company goals
- Self-promotion over company success
- Lack of support from reports

All of these profoundly diminish revenue and profits, as well as the ability to compete successfully in your industry. The bottom line is if you're not willing to help someone else get better, then you're the one who will suffer at the end of the day.

In some ways middle managers have it the hardest—often mid-level executives end up sandwiched between demanding higher executives and lower-level employees or supervisors who fail to perform. These situations tend to create environments in which middle managers in a sense hide out just to hold on to their jobs. Notably, these are people who never raise anyone, and fail to make efforts to do anything more than what they're directly assigned to do. Yet even if they're good at what they do, they'll never get a promotion. They haven't nurtured the capacity to lead.

If compassion for your coworkers is the foundation for business leadership and success, the means by which to express such care is to become an expert in communication. Arrogance and political maneuvering cuts off knowledge. People won't trust you if they think you're only looking out for yourself, so they'll never tell you when the train is heading straight down the tracks in your direction. The inability to communicate effectively is often rooted in a basic lack of consideration toward other people—and it is the seed for tremendous mistrust. If you care about people and you want them to do well—which you do for your own hide, if nothing else—then you have to challenge yourself to communicate as effectively as possible.

I'm not suggesting that it's easy to do this. If you have a dozen people in a room working as many as 10–12 hours a day, there are bound to be conflicts. But a compassionate and considerate leader will see to it that conflicts are addressed and resolved as quickly as possible.

So how do you get out of the mid-management sandwich? Go work with someone else below you. The higher-ups will always notice if they see other people performing well in a previously underperforming department. In fact, this is what senior management is most looking for. To be a top-level leader you need layers of people knowing how to raise others and growing the business. By hiding out, or laying low, you think you're protecting yourself short term, but actually you're hurting yourself long term.

Refrain from practicing politics at work. Politics kills long-term strategy because politicians inherently appeal to the mood of the public in any given moment. In a corporate or business setting, political players generally seek to say what they think is most acceptable to a more limited audience—usually their bosses. If you think this way, you're only thinking of yourself. Moreover, as is made plainly clear by the phenomena of public opinion surveys, poll numbers can rise or fall in seconds.

To be strategic—and, really, to be smart on a long-term basis—you have to include and nurture the workers underneath you to take on the jobs of people moving up or out. And you have to give them clear and thorough feedback.

Millennials couldn't care less if an older manager they don't like anyway isn't moving up in the company. They will march right over you. It's true that older workers will become bitter as they age and watch younger, more capable workers moving past. But why are these Millennials moving up? In part, it's because they've been raised to act in concert with the newer business mores of respect, consideration, and team building. And if the older worker fails to adapt, he or she will be bypassed. I've see this happen all the time.

Older, stuck managers who fail to learn how to communicate and lead resemble battered children. They become defensive, withdrawn, and overreact when their emotional triggers are pulled. There's no path up because the individual didn't do the leadership work when he or she could have. Whether or not you're promoted has nothing to do with age—it's about capability. Indeed, lack of movement due to age is a lame excuse. Why would anyone kick out the door someone good, who happens to be older? The problem with these sorts of managers is they weren't trained to raise people but rather batter them. See how far you'll get badgering Millennials—they'll group together and cut you out so fast your head will spin.

If you don't develop the skills to sit down with someone unhappy or troubled you're going to pay a price. And more than talking, the bigger part of effective communications is *listening*. If you fail to listen, you'll misapprehend the problem—accordingly, whatever solution you come up with will be short term. And if that's all you do, then no one will see you as a long-term leader.

Changing jobs is really tough. I once worked with a corporate lawyer who was let go from his downsizing law firm, and it took him almost three years to get back on his feet. It's emotionally draining, financially devastating, and spiritually challenging to lose a job. Don't let this happen to you because you neglect to understand how businesses are most effectively managed today—take the problem-solving steps described here on the foundation of compassion, and always maintain a long-term view.

The story of Tom, a very competent media executive, will help to illustrate this perspective. Tom had come up "the hard way" and earned everything that he had by his own hard work, ingenuity, and persistence. And he was one of those people who would never take no for an answer. He would stick with something until he figured it out. He had a rough upbringing with two parents who were immigrants from China and spoke very little English. He had to look out for them as much as he had to look out for himself as he grew up and went through college. To this day he still takes an active role in caring for his folks. With this kind of noble character, some might think what a great guy Tom must be. He is, and he is very special mainly because he had the courage to change at 48 years old.

Tom's problem was that he was a tough manager, especially with Millennial-age workers. At one point his entire team went to Tom's boss and threatened to quit if things didn't change. They couldn't take his rigid stance on performance, and especially the way he would deliver the message to them, basically telling them their work was far below average, and how could they possibly think that it would ever be good enough?

The first and most damaging result was that they would never come to him for help. If they didn't know how to do something or were unsure about an outcome, the last thing they wanted to do was to ask Tom for advice. Who would when there was a strong possibility that he would throw you into a meat grinder?!

Needless to say, the long-term result of how Tom mismanaged was far more dangerous. His direct boss and the COO of the company knew how smart and capable Tom was. But what they were not seeing was any of his people taking on more responsibility or getting promoted.

The company was growing rapidly, especially internationally, and they were thinking about Tom taking over the leadership of an international division from which a large percentage of the company's future revenue was going to derive. This particular division needed strong leadership as well as technical expertise, and Tom was the only guy they had with that level of technical prowess.

Naturally Tom knew about this possible promotion, and he wanted it very badly. He had been a middle manager for more than five years, and he was worried about getting stuck at that level. So by the time Tom came to me he was more than discouraged—he was devastated. He was expecting the promotion, and then his team complained about him. Their complaint made it all the way up to the COO, and that killed the promotion. So here was this sad, dejected guy sitting across from me. I told him right away that I thought he could turn all of this around and end up not only with the promotion but also with a supportive team that he could grow into a very capable one.

At that point he thought I was nuts, but there was also a glimmer of hope in his eyes.

We started with what I perceived as his lack of caring. He told me he did care about his workers, and he thought about them a lot. "How do you care for them?" I asked. "You certainly don't show it very well." I told him to put himself in their shoes. How would he feel if he was their age and someone told him his "work sucked," and he didn't know what he was doing?

He said he would be shocked, but he would then try twice as hard. Really? Well, what if you didn't know how to do part of your job, would you feel comfortable going to your boss who told you sucked and ask for help? He was honest and said no. Then we talked about the fact that his workers weren't raised like he was. They, like many Millennials, had never completely depended on themselves. Someone, usually the parents of most Millennial-generation workers, took the tough blows for them and made their path a little too easy in some cases. But so what? They didn't know any different. And how could they? For Tom to be angry with them because they weren't as self-reliant as he was at their age was ridiculous. They didn't know how to do it.

Tom started to see the light. I asked him point-blank if he wanted to learn how to help his workers, or if he wanted to stay angry with them and blow his career out of the water. He got it, and we discussed the best and quickest ways to regain his employees' trust, and how to demonstrate to them that he cared about their work and well-being—a dynamic they were used to and had indeed grown up with from their parents. We focused on how to help them develop their careers. I then took him through the eight steps of creating a career path for Millennials.

I first developed these eight steps in support of a management team perplexed about how to create a clear path for Millennials who had constantly badgered them for promotions. The whole idea is that instead of saying they *can't* have a certain job, you tell them *you will help them* to get the job they want. This then makes you a supporter and an advocate for them—just like what their parents were. Instead of presenting yourself as an enemy, someone who is saying no to them (something they aren't familiar with), you'll get a lot more out of Millennial employees by genuinely reaching out as a friend and mentor.

The emotional trick, of course, is to not show them that you think they're entitled, spoiled brats. Rather, challenge yourself to be supportive. The reason Millennials are the way they are—and there are a lot of them—is that they don't know any better most of the time. I'm not even making a value judgment; it's how they are, and it reflects the cultural mores of doing business today. We can't change how Millennials were raised, and also there's no reason to try to do so—there's a lot of terrific attributes that Millennials possess, not the least of which includes a more refined consideration for people in general.

Following these eight guidelines is a lot less time consuming than compared to the time it takes to deal with Millennials coming into your office asking for some promotion or other advantage—and getting them placated and back to work.

DEVELOPING A CAREER PATH FOR MILLENNIALS

1. Find out which job they want to go after—whether it's vice president, director, or manager level. If they don't know, then ask them to pick one, or else you can't help them get there.
2. On your own, list all of the qualifications that the position requires.

3. Determine what they don't know and will have to learn to get the job (probably all of your aforementioned qualifications).
4. Then meet and tell them you want to help them get the position. (Pause for the shock effect.)
5. Outline for them what the job will take and what you think they will have to learn.
6. Then make a timeline with them pertaining to how long it will take for them to learn what they need to know before they apply (e.g., three months, six months, one year).
7. Create a critical path with them, and for them, including targets, milestones, dates to reach milestones, and finally the end goal of applying for the job.
8. Finally, add when you'll be able to help them. Pick actual times and dates based on your availability. Even if you give them an hour or two a month, they will feel taken care of.

Tom tried this with one of his direct reports and got an incredible result—the employee thanked him profusely and told him that no one had ever taken the time to show him how to develop a plan to get the job he wanted.

The real benefit for Tom was that it made him focus on the employee, not on just what he wanted the guy to do for him. After several weeks of testing this out with some of his other reports, Tom started to nurture a reputation for developing people. This was in three short weeks. After six months of suffering from a horrible reputation as a manager, he had turned his image around in less than a month. Tom got the international promotion, which automatically doubled the size of his team.

So what were the several techniques that Tom learned to help him to become a successful manager? These included how to effectively and genuinely communicate through departmental meetings, e-mails, phone calls, and one-on-one conversations; the explanation of complex problems through the use of simple words and concepts; the use of confident body language; doing himself what he asked others to do; encouraging feedback; and, perhaps most importantly, showing appreciation. Underneath all this were the goals of problem solving, the development of genuine compassion, and the design of critical paths for project team members.

All of these techniques helped Tom to lead and manage more effectively. But the greatest thing he learned was that he had the power to change himself. He gave that gift to himself when he decided to overcome the leadership issues he was facing. He's a courageous guy, and one I have a lot of respect for. I don't care what anybody says, it really is never too late to change and have a positive impact on the careers of others and especially your own. It just takes guts.

Does all this mean that every person is a valuable resource? Well, yes and no. Every person has the potential and capacity to be capable, but the truth is that the right person in the right position is the most valuable resource. It's axiomatic that poor managers will lead deficient organizations, and that compassionate, smart, and hard-working leaders will perform better. But it's also clear that everyone will work harder, and profits will increase, if we care about each person assigned as our reports.

In Buddhism, again, it's said that the capacity for enlightenment is equivalent to how much we care for others. We're not shooting for anything as abstract as enlightenment in a business setting, of course, but the concept still applies. When we care for others who report to us, our own business strength increases. As a result, our profits increase, because we're cutting waste from our business environments by helping people to work more effectively and happily. Actions to benefit others are not separate from actions to benefit ourselves. This is because, as observed earlier, our lives and the lives of others are inseparable—the concept, again, of dependent origination. And in a business environment, where a department is striving toward a common goal, it's even more true than in virtually any other aspect of life.

An attitude of compassion, by the way, doesn't mean looking down on someone, or pitying them for their lack of business savvy or skills. Instead, compassion is based on respect. Indeed what business needs today more than ever—and what the Millennials, for all their various differences, generally bring to our business environments—is empathy. Empathy is the ability to put ourselves in the shoes of our coworkers who are struggling, to understand and share what they're going through. I know this is a radical concept, especially in light of the celebratory plaudits offered by our contemporary media to individuals like Donald Trump, who appear to embody opposite goals. But I will assure you this is exactly where successful companies are heading. When the spirit of compassion, or empathy, becomes the bedrock of doing business, and is embodied by top corporate leaders, I believe the profitability and efficiency of American corporations will skyrocket.

Chapter 5

The Notion of Strategic Compassion

Building Trust and Creating Value through an Enlightened Leadership

The Dalai Lama once said that if you must be selfish, be wisely selfish. What he means is that there's a big difference between being destructive as compared to performing self-interested good deeds. Both, in a sense, are selfish acts, but the latter will create value for yourself and others, while the former will result only in loss.

Strategic compassion, at its essence, is the idea that your career and leadership skills will advance to the extent that you empathize with and help others with whom you work to become more skilled and productive. In turn, your business will grow in profitability. Being strategically humanistic, of course, is just a more effective way to compete. It's a method to win in the tough parts of business, and at the end of the day it boosts your bottom line. These skills are essential to becoming a successful entrepreneur and business owner.

If you have your own business, you're going to have to lead it. And, as we've learned, you can't lead unless people trust you. To put it bluntly, you won't be effective unless you control your own self-regard and instead learn how to make others a priority. It takes courage to honestly get to know what's going on with your coworkers. And believe me, there's a difference between thinking you're the kind of person who can do this versus actually doing it. For example, playing with a flight simulator on your computer isn't flying an airplane. To be strategically compassionate means to not be self-centered. It means to first look at what the *other* person's concerns are, not *yours*. Know what's going on with people. Know their objectives and acknowledge them. You build trust by helping them achieve their goals and become better at their jobs by supporting the process of strengthening and improving themselves.

Strategic compassion is based on the fact that an unhappy or unskilled worker not only is not productive but individually costly and a drain on profit. The presence of unhappy workers means it costs more to get what you want done. Profit margins improve, of course, when people work more efficiently, and they work efficiently when they're happy and satisfied. The lack of productive individuals, moreover, often hurts a larger department as a whole. These workers will increase toxicity in the workplace; their negativity spreads. No one wants to talk to them, and that costs you a fortune. You then become a manager trying to fix the problem rather than being a leader. As soon as you're running around with a fire extinguisher you're not leading. You're just plugging holes. And, like Whack-A-Mole, there will always be another problem popping out of another hole.

Negative workers can pull down the positive spirit of other people. The key to defusing such situations and turning these people around is found by acknowledging that they're upset without, at first, worrying about why or whether their complaints are justified. Accept them as they are, justified or not. If you deny them, whether because of logic or defensiveness, they're just going to get more upset and will avoid you. All people are like this—we all get upset one way or another.

WHAT'S THE CAUSE OF THE UPSET?

Anger is usually the byproduct of frustration and a feeling of powerlessness. It's almost always undirected and unrestrained. Many times it's projected anger and falsely directed. We all have it, but few of us recognize it for what it is—a rogue and renegade force, disrupting and destroying all in its path. Angry people aren't able to see things clearly or attack the true issues or problems at work. Anger affects their judgment, makes them defensive, and their priorities suddenly become placating their anger and projecting blame instead of getting the work done. The inner distortions twisting the heart of someone in this state prevent him or her from seeing things in his or her true aspect or making correct judgments. Everything appears as a means to the fulfillment of egotistical desires and impulses. Anger is an uncontrolled, emotional reaction or trigger that can cause a tremendous amount of damage.

Showing someone respect is the first step in deescalating a situation and dealing with such anger. The ability to embrace and not shun someone who is angry controls the damage. Communicating skillfully and appropriately so as to foster acceptance has a great impact not only on security but also on productivity in the workplace. An important point to always keep in mind is that anger does more harm to the angry person than to anyone toward whom that anger is directed.

There's a wise saying, often attributed to the Buddha, that anger is like drinking poison and expecting the other person to die. Stay calm, and be aware of your triggers. You have the power to help someone out of this situation. Once your own house is in order, you can then listen carefully to the other person's concerns. If you're thinking that this #$%*#@ really pisses me off, I have to calm him down, you've lost. People's intuitions are so highly tuned, especially when emotional, they'll pick it up. They'll know if you're just trying to placate them. You'll have no credibility. You have to mean it if you want to help them. Otherwise, they'll remain upset and walk away mad.

Most importantly, you have to understand your own emotional triggers—that's the only way to help someone with theirs. The goal is to build trust through the heated situation and thereby create value from the obstacle. Obstacles can be opportunities that may create success. The smooth stuff is easy.

I recall working with a 62-year-old supervisor named Tom who, throughout his career, had anger-management difficulties. His entire team resented him, and in turn he'd blow up at them to such an extent that it nearly led to fist fights. I encouraged him to change his approach. By this I mean that I trained him to have his team take on projects that he explained were important to him but, instead of shouting, to let them know that he really needed each of them and depended on them. By showing them respect, in a sincere way, they took responsibility and stopped complaining. And they did this even without the carrot of a promotion or raise. In turn, Tom learned what his emotional triggers were and how to control them. Frankly, it was a challenge for a guy like him to change his behavior so late in his career. But the upshot was that his team's performance increased by 35 percent. Moreover, in emergencies, his department's supervising vice president would go straight to Tom to ask him to handle them—bypassing Tom's director and manager.

So how do you get someone who is acting out to take responsibility for their actions? The cardinal rule, as a leader, is that you can't lose control. You have to rein in your own emotions; if you lack the ability to do this, people become nervous. They think the driver isn't driving the bus. This is where you have to be strong. There's no magic wand; there's no resident psychiatrist on call. Instead, you have to know and manage yourself. Remember your trigger words.

The outcome of whatever happens, and however someone feels, is up to you. It's you, not them—you control the outcome of the situation. Many times it has nothing to do with the situation in front of you; rather the anger is triggered by something that happened a long time ago. How are you going to respond next? What's your trigger? Understand what they're experiencing, and then think of a word that reminds you of your past triggers. Whatever it might be, write it on a notepad or smartphone and look at it before you speak or act. This will help you to remember the new behavior you're trying to implement in your interactions with others.

Rather than avoidance, embracing the person in his or her angry state is the key to gain enough trust to learn what's actually going on. This takes some resilience. You need to have courage to do this—if you don't have it, you need to build it. Some people are angry because they care about their job and aren't able to do it well. If that's the case, acknowledge it instead of putting it, or that person, down.

Listening is the biggest key to defusing anger, which itself is not necessarily a bad thing. If someone's angry, at least it shows that they care. But you want to get beneath that anger and learn how to analyze the real interests involved.

It's easy to get flustered or upset when you're confronted with an angry person; and, if you don't know how to respond, you can easily make the situation worse. Millennial-generation coworkers, in particular, present peculiar challenges of their own, and it's worth exploring these in some detail.

Let's face it—a lot of Millennials are spoiled and have been raised by so-called helicopter parents who fight their kids' battles for them—and, as a result, yes they tend to feel entitled. Many kids in the most recent generation never had to "get up off the mat" and have had limited opportunities to engage in a struggle. It could be said, rather, that many have been rewarded for not doing much.

Accordingly, people tend to resent Millennials when they act spoiled and entitled. But if you're in a leadership position, your issue isn't so much whether the Millennial feels entitled but instead how to deal with the coworkers who might feel resentment toward him or her. The way to overcome both the shortcomings of certain Millennials and the hostility they occasionally, and unintentionally, engender is to work closely with them to create their career paths.

Millennials tend to want or expect to be promoted to vice president after two months on the job, so show them how to get there and what it's going to take. That's using logos—they can't argue with logic. Moreover, you've now shown interest in them (which they're used to), and you've given them a good dose of reality as far as advancement is concerned. You're no longer the guy denying them what they want but instead you're helping them to get it. The true picture, so to speak, throws a little water on their fire; in any case, you've helped them to see things as they really are. The key is to say you're going to help them to get there—and mean it. Then, you're not just coddling, but you're embracing them.

Show your Millennial coworker the steps to succeed in your business, and specifically outline for them what they have to know and do. This, in turn, is a subtle way of revealing what they don't know. Anchor them in the reality of what a vice president for operations, for example, actually does. If they see themselves as a senior manager and think they deserve to achieve that position quickly, then specifically outline that job description for them and what they will have to be able to do to succeed at the position. Then it's not personal—it becomes a rational and logical process, rather than *they want it but you're not giving it to them.* Explain to them that many people never professionally recover from being raised too rapidly. And engaging them in the process like this shows them your concern. Help the Millennial worker, in particular, to design his or her own career path so they know what to do to get what they want. This not only disarms arrogance, but it also instills effective work habits.

I recently worked with a 33-old business development executive named James. This man wanted to have a Ferrari and everything that came with it before he was 31. He was smart, very aggressive, and an excellent salesman. James also upset almost everyone he worked with, being overly demanding and expecting everyone to support him without investing in them. Yet he couldn't understand why he wasn't a vice president already. He knew he needed to change something, so he came to me for coaching.

I showed him what all of the responsibilities of a senior executive in his industry would entail. Then I asked him how he would perform the first two of these. Naturally he had no idea—so he tried to guess and just dug himself into a deeper hole. Then I told him the right answers, and he immediately realized he didn't have either the knowledge or experience that the job would require. He was *very* discouraged. But I immediately engaged him in making a plan for learning what he would need to know to advance in his career. We went through the necessary leadership skills, business skills, and industry knowledge that he would have to accumulate over the next year or two. He was very relieved to see clearly an actual path to follow and could not wait to get started.

I then spoke to him as he would speak to the people that worked for him and with him. He stammered and stumbled trying to answer my questions. I then asked him how that felt—he got the message right away. To his credit, he perceived how to put himself in the other person's shoes before he would ask him or her to do something or make demands on him or her. James has since learned many new leadership skills, and the people who work with him have told him directly that they see and appreciate the major change in him. The CEO and COO of the company both have told me that they're thrilled with how he's changed.

In every case, when you respond calmly and with empathy, you can stay in control, and you can defuse any situation in a professional, courteous way.

Critically, you can't succumb to whatever triggers your own anger. By doing this, you break the emotional spirals of escalation, and you can solve the underlying problems that have caused their anger—especially since such people have probably reacted this way their entire lives. The truth is that if you respond forcefully to someone else's anger, you can easily end up being seen as the aggressor yourself. Obviously, this is disastrous in a business context and will destroy the bonds of trust you've worked to establish. In fact, responding well to angry people ultimately builds positive relationships with them. If you get angry and beat on them, then you've become the bully. Trust is critical. When someone is losing it, and you neither abandon nor attack him or her, they defuse themselves and learn they can always come to you. This protects your business from further damage. It enables you to nip problems in the bud, saving money, time, and clients. Moreover, when you respond calmly to angry episodes, you set a good example for others. Your behavior will inspire the people around you, which can transform a team's ability to work even more productively.

Most critically, you're creating the culture of your department and company. Your future leaders and managers are learning how to act in a way that will also create value for the company. That's worth its weight in gold. People will respect you when you don't freak out. This will transform and enable a team to be self-correcting. That will save time—and money—as well.

Matrix management means the ability to work with other departments. It's managing without direct authority. It's the practice of managing individuals with more than one reporting line, but it also describes managing cross-functional, cross-business group and other forms of working that cross the traditional vertical business units of function and geography. A successful manager seeks to manage others who he or she does not have direct authority over. Over such a broad and sometimes attenuated structure, seek input from workers in order to understand that division's process, what they need, how the person you're working with likes to do things. Learn their micro-culture. Then you'll know how to approach them, you'll know how they work. Don't worry about them caring about how you work—they don't. You're the one who wants to build trust and lead, but you have to do this tactically. Don't tell them what you need; instead, find out first what they need and enfold those needs within your larger vision. In other words, don't try to change the deck of cards, but rather work with what you're dealt.

Understand your people, understand your business environment, and deal with it all in a compassionate, logical, and rational way without misleading anyone. Don't avoid issues that will do nothing but blow up down the line.

The solution to the challenges of bad news or hurt feelings is found in the nexus of intelligence and compassion—within logic, rationality, and honesty. This leads to consideration. This approach takes courage. And you have to realize we're talking about lasting change, not a quick fix. It's not about being cool—it's a lifelong change. It's about integrity and being dependable. Gossip and misinformation and problems that are not dealt with quickly lead to disruption. Disruption leads to inefficiency, higher costs, lower profits, and higher stress. The result of a strategically compassionate approach can create tremendous value—in fact, it nurtures a value deeper than the point of any one business. There are going to be people who really rub you the wrong way. You may not like a particular worker but you're making an effort on his or her behalf, which pushes you, precipitates your personal growth, and also benefits the company.

But if you apply strategic compassion as a manipulative tool, people will see through it. Engineers with the master degrees and PhDs are very smart, but the intuition of the workers on the factory floor can be sharper. Their intuition can be more highly developed than that of an educated person. When Enron folded, for example, the employee stock was locked, and the stock was thereafter dumped. Meanwhile, Kenneth Lay and the other top executives had the freedom to sell their stock. Yet Lay and the others cynically tried to reassure their employees, publicly, that they knew how they felt because they took a hit too. It tanked. It's not that Lay was stupid—rather, he was not in tune with the people who worked for him. He had only his own selfish interests on his mind. Ultimately, that is real stupidity.

The founder of Alibaba, Jack Ma, on the other hand, didn't necessarily understand the nuances of his tech business but was extremely knowledgeable about both the Chinese market and the customs of the 3,000-year-old culture in which he established his business. Moreover, the key issue in China was trust. What he did to overcome the trust issue was to hold the payment in escrow until the person received the goods. That's how he grew the business.

There always has to be some risk or stakes on the table—as Ma famously said, "Today is cruel. Tomorrow is crueler. And the day after tomorrow is beautiful."

This is not easy. If you want to remain an individual contributor I understand completely. If you want to just manage and be happy with that, that's fine too. Being a leader requires extra effort and dedication, passion, and most importantly requires you to care about other people. Leadership is service. If you can't do this, you can't lead. If you're willing to do it, the rewards are beyond compare and limitless.

I once worked with two executives in a large, healthcare service business. Healthcare is a tough market, and the competition is fierce. One executive was really good and hardworking, and his people liked him. The other tended to get frustrated when someone didn't do something right. Both were intelligent and well educated—in fact, both were medical doctors. But one of them would habitually pound people, and then try to justify the behavior by saying "I just hope you understand that I want it right." But, you know what? People still didn't trust that person because he's rationalizing bad behavior to make it acceptable to himself. Where's the recognition of the other person's humanity in that?

You can't lead unless people trust you. When things are going well, everything will be fine, but when you hit a rough patch, and you're not trusted, you'll find that no one will be following. Think about what you yourself like and want. Don't you love it when people ask what's going on, what your major concerns are? Don't you feel good when someone pays attention to you? If someone trusts you, it's because they know you have their concerns at heart. You have to see their concerns before your own. This isn't self-negating, it's the wisdom of how to do business.

In a matrix environment you have to pull people together to accomplish goals, because you don't have direct authority. But how do you do this when they have a zillion other things pulling at them? How do you become the fire that needs to be put out?

One young guy I know in the technology business, a relatively senior manager, came across a situation in which five different corporate departments each were analyzing the same business matter independently. It struck him that the five departments ought to perform the analysis together. When he suggested the idea, the resistance was overwhelming. In response, he went around to each head of the respective departments over a five-week period—so as not to appear too obvious—to speak with them about their work, to determine their primary goals, and to find out what their pressures were. He then took that information and tied the benefit of doing the analysis across the board to the individual pressures on each department head—in other words, he translated it for them. As a result, each department head ultimately was persuaded that it was in his or her best interest to work together in a less burdensome way.

You can move to the top of the business food chain by knowing what the other person's primary worry and concern is and helping them to solve it. If you can't help, then at least acknowledge it so they have someone whose ear they can bend. Put the time into them. Put the time in now, and get the long-lasting return later. Permanent, valuable relationships are the key, not something temporary to get through a project. Strategic compassion has nothing to do with weakness. Rather, it's about developing the strength to show concern.

Chapter 6

There's No Such Thing as a Safe Place

The Difference between Leading and Managing

There are essentially two limitations in any interpersonal dynamic—theirs and yours. A great manager is not necessarily a good leader. For example, you might be a terrific and highly valued management tactician but have poor insight and intuition about people. This is not to say that a talented manager has no role in a company—of course he or she does. But a leader is the most valuable commodity a business can possess. And a leader is what the vast majority of Millennials seek in their quest for workplace satisfaction.

Leaders balance technical knowledge and skills with emotional intelligence. Leading means you're going somewhere, you're taking people somewhere new—it's about getting things done. People look toward dynamic leadership to see and prepare them for what's around the corner, to see what's coming. Others are willing to grow because you're growing—seeing that, they feel inspired to do so too.

Every innovation is made because someone did not accept a generalized limitation. You have to learn to get out front and lead, and people need to see it. You have to grow ahead of the curve, not with it. A genuine and successful leader evolves by overcoming personal limitations, seeking mentors, and studying and developing the ability to critically think. In business, there's no such thing as a safe place. Think of it as a flowing river: the current moves you either forward or backward—you're never staying in the same place. A neutral position doesn't exist; life and time themselves are continuous. As George C. Scott, playing General George Patton in the movie *Patton*, said, "I don't want to get any messages saying that 'we are holding our position.' We're not holding anything. . . . We are advancing constantly." Or, as the real Patton said, "I don't like paying for the same real estate twice."

There are a million good managers and very few good leaders. Again, I'm not saying talented managers aren't critical to success—of course they are, and their experiences both in business and from serving in higher positions are vital. But great leaders can appear from anywhere—they can be the lowest guy in the machine shop, or the concierge in the showroom. I see this all the time. I'll walk into a company and sometimes find that the administrative staff is leading everyone.

Recently I had been working quite a lot as a coaching consultant at a large tech company, and I became familiar with many of the top management staff. One young woman in particular stood out to me—her level of maturity and the way others talked with her cast her naturally in a leadership light. One day, after a particularly challenging coaching session with a mid-level executive, I approached her and suggested she needed to admonish a particular individual for certain behavior I'd learned he was engaged in at the office on a regular basis. She sort of looked at me in a bemused way and agreed to take care of it. Later I was told by the company CEO that this woman was no more than an administrative assistant. But he liked that I viewed her as a leader, as did he—and because of this episode, she ended up getting a raise!

So you can find leaders anywhere, but you have to train them in business acumen and consideration. A smart person will go to someone with leadership potential and encourage him or her to get other people to move. Such savvy executives might not even have the ability to do this themselves, but the talented ones recognize this and so identify and then nurture those in their companies who do. Simply put, to find and develop a leader in your organization is the most valuable investment that you can make. And while not many of them especially qualify as such, Millennials in general see themselves as possessing leadership potential. And they are eager to be placed in an environment to display whatever talents they may have in this regard.

At its essence, what constitutes a leader is someone who can and is willing to understand other human beings. You hear so many times people who don't want to manage others, but they certainly want the salary associated with a management position. Still, they don't want to deal with the nitty-gritty of leading a team because they don't know how to do it.

This is also the case with what I refer to as humanistic leadership or strategic compassion—few know how to do it, because no one's taught anyone to do it. Likewise, just because you've managed a dozen people doesn't mean you can manage 50. A capable manager will hold everything to a budget and timeline, they have the nuts and bolts down, but as soon as something goes off the rails, the leadership skills aren't necessarily there to get everyone back on track.

With respect to those Millennials banging on your door and asking for promotions and more responsibilities—you'll either train them to succeed or spend time every week calming them down. The latter is managing the problem, but you're not leading anyone anywhere. Rather, a leader is willing to understand other people, pay attention to other's needs, and put himself or herself in a supporting position with the understanding that the team's success all comes back to him or her at the conclusion of a successful project. And to do this you can't be focused on yourself—you can't lead someone somewhere unless you're totally focused on them.

One of the more conspicuous examples of leadership was embodied by Nelson Mandela. Mandela was a guy who, early in life, was pretty close to what we today would call a terrorist. When he was young, he placed bombs on rail lines that served the then-in-power whites and overtly sought the overthrow of the apartheid government. Eventually he was sent away to a notorious prison for 27 years. While there, he read, and he suffered, and he developed great insight into the nature of people. When the events of the day led to his release in 1990, and his miraculous elevation to the South African presidency, he did something not only unexpected but upsetting to many of his supporters—he went almost immediately to meet with and embrace the leaders of the minority whites and dealt with their needs before the needs even of his black supporters. Ultimately he was hailed for this—he understood that people are just people and that racism is something that is taught.

Mandela's emotional intelligence was so highly developed by the time he was released from prison. And there are many other, albeit less famous, leaders in contemporary business today. Richard Branson, the founder of the Virgin Group, is one. Tony Hsieh, the CEO of Zappos—a 4,000-employee shoe company—has implemented a terrific open culture that's fun and wildly profitable. For a look at a different way of doing things, consider the core corporate values that Zappos publicly touts:

- Deliver WOW through Service
- Embrace and Drive Change
- Create Fun and a Little Weirdness
- Be Adventurous, Creative, and Open-Minded
- Pursue Growth and Learning
- Build Open and Honest Relationship with Communication

- Build a Positive Team and Family Spirit
- Do More with Less
- Be Passionate and Determined
- Be Humble

Isn't this a place you'd love to spend your workday in?

In one sense, you might say that Millennials are looking for parenting—they're craving in a leader someone compassionate and willing to care. Also they want to support supervisors who inspire and offer them respect. They don't think it's necessary or even wise to follow someone who appears to them to be selfish. They'll look at you almost like the temporary help—or something curious but ancient, like a dinosaur. You've got to give real consideration to whether you're building loyalty and trust with them. If you're not, and if accordingly they're not inspired, Millennials will fall back into their selfish modes—they'll ignore you, work less efficiently, and eventually leave your company.

A leader is looking to the future. A manager is dealing with the present.

Looking around the corner includes knowing what's coming, the ability to communicate where you're going, an appreciation and understanding for the people you have, the wisdom to know who can do it well, and the determination to assist those who need help. The leader will consider who's following him or her around the bend; the manager will just want to get the job done. The leader will see opportunities and throw the ball down the field; the manager will just follow the playbook.

A leader can capitalize on crisis; a manager sees crisis as a problem to be fixed. As is widely referenced, the Chinese character for crisis is composed of two characters: one meaning "danger," the other "opportunity" or "critical point"—in other words, it can go either way. Someone's crisis is another person's opportunity. It all depends on your perspective. Again, I'm not knocking managers, because without them the trains don't run on time. Some people are outstanding managers, and they may not want to be leaders. But if you want to float to the top and build something that will last, you have to lead and not manage.

Let's analogize to youth or Little League baseball: some coaches are more concerned about teaching the children how to play; others want to win the game at all costs. Who is the leader in this case, and who is the manager? What would you care most about—developing long term the kids you're managing or getting through the game? That's the difference between leadership and management.

People in business are often used as pawns. But if you coddle Millennials you'll spend so much time flattering them and less training them to be competent at work. If you're not direct with Millennial workers—albeit in a respectful, considerate way—they'll never learn how to bounce back from adversity. Don't placate your workers, and don't shy away. If you smooth it over and just maintain the status quo, then the worker sits there and thinks he or she is okay. Everything's fine until things don't work out—the people who've been treated like this are in shock when they're fired.

Some of the worst business management tactics I've seen are in the American corporate law sector. Most of these firms are partnerships, at least on paper, but the senior partners are essentially managing their own staffs without concern for their partners in the larger economic picture of the law firm enterprise. One department might be booming, while another department runs a money-losing operation. But these firms will rarely move associate attorneys from one practice group to another, and as a result sometimes the entire firm fails. But the heads of these large firms—often led by neither leaders nor even good managers—will schmooze and flatter their junior attorneys only to keep them engaged until they find someone better. Then they fire them. It's not only a woeful reflection of inefficient management that cuts unnecessarily into the firm's profits, but it's weak and lacks courage.

Lawyers are highly educated, very sophisticated and yet many of them can't effectively lead their own firms. Intelligence does not predict leadership. Yet the truth is that the world is run by leaders, not managers.

Managers are often resented—workers never put out their best efforts for them. Leaders, on the other hand, are followed. Leaders trust their reports. They set forth the vision, and they ask them to get it done. And when it does get done, and done well, the leaders first give credit to the team members who did the work. A sign of strong leadership is when a person's reports are so developed that in a crisis they will pick up the ball and run with it. The leader, concentrating on training even more people, develops the capacity to trust others so much, and be available for them when needed, that the people under him work as hard as he or she does.

A true leader never takes credit for someone else's work—he or she always turns and gives them the credit, and builds them up. They don't steal their team members' credit. When you're capable of acknowledging others in this way, you're building incredible trust with people—this is especially true in the case of Millennial workers, who often expect such credit.

One of the great historical examples of excellent corporate leadership is to be found with Johnson & Johnson. In 1982 seven people in Chicago died tragically after taking Tylenol capsules that had been laced with cyanide. Johnson & Johnson immediately launched a public relations campaign to save not only its brand but its corporation as a whole. Tylenol as a product appeared to be doomed.

At great financial loss, the company alerted the American public not to consume any Tylenol products. Moreover, it recalled approximately 31 million bottles of Tylenol, worth more than $100 million. Further, Johnson & Johnson offered to exchange all Tylenol capsules that had already been purchased—millions of bottles more—with Tylenol tablets. And it did all this with the knowledge that there were probably no other bottles containing cyanide anywhere else in the country. Finally, the company rolled out new batches of product—millions of bottles more—bearing the first tamper-resistant packaging in the nation. Why did it take such a huge loss? To both protect its customers and preserve its corporate reputation.

The leaders of the company at the time of course were not prepared for a business disaster of this magnitude. But interestingly, credit for a campaign that was attributed for saving Johnson & Johnson's good name was given to a corporate credo expressed by Robert Wood Johnson II, the leader of the company way back in the 1940s, that set forth the notion that the company must have a responsibility to society going far beyond profit motive. In other words, a credo bearing a long-term vision that was both moral and profitable is what saved Johnson & Johnson 40 years later. That's leadership—both in Johnson's case to foresee it, and in the case of the corporate leaders decades later who relied on it.

Leaders take the hit if something goes wrong; managers often will blame their staff. If you're managing Millennials, try doing that once or twice and see how many hang around. Millennials are a tribe—mess with a few of them, and they will all start looking for a new job. And think about this: In the next 10 years 75 percent of the American workforce will be Millennial workers. If you're leading and looking around the corner, you had better know that this is coming.

In contrast to Johnson & Johnson, Enron, and to some extent some other large corporations with diminishing technologies or increasingly disreputable products, offers examples of failing businesses grounded in greed and selfishness. Enron is of course a celebrated example of a failed corporate culture with massive ethical defects. Enron's senior management, among other major failures, neglected to maintain a relationship of openness and trust with its employees. People who complained were ignored, silenced, or fired. Senior management cared much more about self-enrichment than it did for the needs of its employees. This toxic culture of corporate greed resulted in a massive damage to the U.S. economy, as well as long prison sentences for Enron's corporate leaders.

If you want to be a leader of Millennials, you have to be honest and take responsibility. Otherwise you won't get anywhere with them. You might get something *out* of them but the long-term result will be low morale and revenue loss.

There's a famous Buddhist saying that one tall tree does not make a forest. Unless other trees grow to the same height, you can't develop a large grove. The true worth of a leader rests on one thing: how many people have you fostered to carry your vision forward?

Again, a manager's job is to organize and coordinate. A leader's role is to plan, inspire, and motivate. A manager lights a fire under people. A leader lights a fire inside of people. The manager repeats observed behaviors; the leader originates. In the Millennial economy, value comes from the development of people. Keep your employees happy, and do not treat them as mere cogs in a machine.

Build your team by inspiring each member of the team to share in the group's goal. The key here is to attune their personal objectives at work to the overarching vision of the group or company. Team building is the process by which you achieve this through solving tasks and interpersonal conflicts that affect team functionality.

For example, if someone feels frustrated at a task, for whatever reason, consider coupling that person with someone who's good at that particular job. Even better, try to pair people with complementary strengths and weaknesses. This is great for team building because you're promoting the sharing of information. And constantly keep it rotating so that there's a fresh exchange of ideas.

I coached someone once who was interested in leaving an engineering firm for a larger and more reputable one. She researched the new company, studied everything she could find about the CEO, knew exactly what they were doing, and had practically memorized the CEO's life story. This is where knowledge is powerful—they hired her. So she joins this new team and is given a new project. But she knew her success wasn't only predicated on knowledge—she recognized the importance of getting to know her colleague well, and so she started to invite different individuals to lunch to ask about the company, and also to ask about them. At the end, she came up with a new idea on something they had been doing one way forever. She found a more efficient way—but that meant a lot of people who were there for a long time would have to do something a different way. She was afraid to bring it up, but I told her to go ahead because she had a ton of support after becoming friends with everyone. So she got her courage up and pitched the idea and 90 percent of the people supported it because they thought it was a good idea, but also because they liked her. That's someone who's going somewhere in her company.

The term "knowledge worker" was first coined by the great management expert Peter Drucker in the late 1950s. The following excerpt from his work *Management Challenges in the 21st Century* demonstrated particular foresight:

> Increasingly "employees" have to be managed as "partners"—and it is the definition of a partnership that all partners are equal. It is also the definition of a partnership that partners cannot be ordered. They have to be persuaded. . . . One

does not "manage" people. The task is to lead people. And the goal is to make productive the specific strengths and knowledge of each individual.

So what happens when you don't actually practice what you preach? I recall an excellent example of a one-time vice president for human resources at a large company. He held himself out as the "well-being guy" at his firm. He even maintained a blog about treating people well, offering suggestions about how to make sure employees are well cared for. He preached all of this as a mid-level HR guy, and honestly that helped to secure for him the inside track on his eventual promotion to head of the department.

So, as one might expect, the first thing he did was to meet with the existing directors and managers—the people that he once worked with who now would be reporting to him. The idea of these meetings, of course, would be to solicit their thoughts about how the department had been running and their suggestions about how its business might be more efficient or otherwise improved. But people immediately noticed a few alarming things—the meetings were brief, and in many instances the new VP spent his time looking at his smartphone while his staff offered their opinions. Then, without circling back to consult, he set forth an agenda that marked a relatively radical departure from how the department, which had been otherwise successful, had been run. But many of these staff members had been there for years. In other words, the VP had just fired the opening salvo of what was soon to become a culture of mistrust. Most importantly, instead of researching exactly where things stood at the company, he laid out his own plan and insisted that everyone follow it—and he held himself out as an experienced HR guy!

People invested in the success of this department didn't know what to do. Soon enough, he brought in people from outside the company—people with whom he'd worked with before—and they started to dictate to those already there about what to do. Eventually of course the older staff started to push back. They had been there for years, and they know what was needed. The VP responded by meeting with these older directors and managers, who he perceived as unsupportive, to complain that they weren't on board. The response they offered was that they fully wanted to support him but that he hadn't bothered to tell them what was expected of them.

The next day he called the same people in and fired them. Others quit—they knew quickly that things were going south. So by now the VP had alienated himself from the other remaining directors in the department, and they didn't want to work with him. He brought in more of his own people, and then constantly changed job descriptions in an attempt to protect his own turf. And all this time he carried himself off as holistic leader! He even denied certain benefits to people about to have a baby!

I did meet finally meet with this executive. And he did reveal to me what he ultimately wanted to achieve. I can't say that his vision was flawed, but the ways he went about his business I found to be disastrous. Maybe I just perceived him as an overt hypocrite, but I have to say this was one of the few times in my career that I almost hesitated to give someone the tools they needed to succeed. In the end that didn't much matter—soon enough he was indeed fired, costing the company a significant amount of money.

In the end, the COO had to get into the middle of the HR department and personally interview the staff to find out what was going on—and this is a COO of a very large corporation with a lot more pressing matters to have to deal with. The fired VP left a mess—lawsuits were fired for wrongful termination, and ultimately a lot of the outside people he brought in were let go as well.

In the aftermath of his departure I observed that cause and effect is strict. I encouraged the affected people not to hold onto their anger; this guy, one way or another, would experience his just desserts.

As a final note to the story, I several weeks later happened to have lunch with the head of a big entertainment organization. He knew I was consulting with this other corporation and happened to ask what was going on over there. I told the story, in general terms, about the guy who was fired. What would you think were the first words out of his mouth? He wanted to know the guy's name. The point is that the effect indeed follows the cause. One way or another word would get out about this individual, and he'd be very unlikely to find work again at that level in that particular city. And all this because this VP failed to genuinely ask his staff what they thought.

Julie, a mid-level manager at a media buying company, offers on the other hand an example of how to do things the right way.

Julie was newly promoted to a position for managing a group that writes various proposals. She came up through the ranks and, after her promotion, found herself with 10 direct reports. She was worried about how to gain authority, as well as their respect, since she was not long ago one of them—but now she's the boss. She wanted to be viewed as the leader, and indeed she did know her stuff. She told me her people were overworked, all very young, and generally stressed—and that most of them had started at this company. For all of them, it was a first real job, and there was a lot of on-the-job learning. The company was growing, and there was a lot of pressure to make it work—under such conditions, a lack of experience starts to show.

As happens at times, she found herself in a position of having to correct people when they were wrong, and in one instance she had to let someone go. She felt as if she was the one giving out bad news all the time. She said that her staff loved to work, and they're young with lots of energy, but that the main problem in her view was that they don't know if that the job was what they wanted to end up doing—she'd often hear that "this not what I envisioned for my career." That's a typical Millennial view. These workers, of course, wanted to keep their jobs, but they were just not sure and accordingly were unmotivated. How would she ever get people like this on board to work efficiently together?

The key issue is to always go to the root cause of the problem. What was the key challenge? Their inexperience. Employees that lack experience or knowledge can be taught what they need to know to be successful.

The root of the issue was their lack of interest in learning new things. You have to show your workers the value of *being able* to learn something new, and adapt. So Julie had to coach them to learn to do a task well from the perspective of challenging oneself to develop skills that would be very useful later in their career. Her industry wouldn't be the same a year from now anyway—the key skill for any worker is to learn, adapt, and take on new things. That's itself a highly valued skill. A typical American will enjoy at least a 40-year long career. How much have things changed in 40 years? How vital is it, obviously, to develop an ability to be able to learn something new?

Instead of sitting around saying you can't do it, or it's not my cup of tea—learn how to do the task in front of you. The ability to adapt will pay off because industry is constantly changing, and you have to learn how to learn. So Julie showed them the importance of learning the job that they already had. It didn't matter to them at the end whether they became expert proposal writers—what was way more valuable was the satisfaction in knowing that they could adapt to whatever was placed before them. Most of Julie's staff completely turned around. Most of them even studied on their own time to learn how to do their jobs better. Basically, she left it up to them, but they were motivated and inspired because they recognized that it was for their benefit. That's strategic compassion.

Millennials are young, they've grown up with change, they're used to it, they've seen technology advance rapidly in their lives. So take an element from their culture and show them that it's an actual skill set. Now they see Julie as someone looking out for them, rather than someone critiquing them. Their attitude changed because she came at it from a different direction.

Lead who you have to lead. Whomever is there is who you're supposed to work with. If you engage with them, the ones who don't belong there eventually will self-select out.

A young guy I coached named Larry was an ex-military guy, very tough and disciplined guy with a huge work responsibility overseeing the manufacture of critical aircraft components. But his entire staff was comprised of individuals without military experience and lacking even close to the self-discipline with which Larry conducted his affairs. I ended up coaching him because his team was angry at him, hiding from him, complaining about him because he kept making people work too much. The company liked him a lot, but all the complaints against him were causing problems both for him and his department.

He was very perplexed and couldn't grasp why his workers simply wouldn't do what they were supposed to do. Why did he always have to badger them? He would tell them clearly what they needed to do, and within how much time, and they would constantly fail to meet deadlines. They would find reasons why they couldn't do whatever was assigned. So, as good managers would do, he would get in and do it himself, but in the process, and although not intended, embarrass them and put them down. That was his management style—again that's managing, not leading. Plus they were afraid to talk to him, as if he was Mr. Perfect and they were losers. (He was pretty close to being Mr. Perfect too.)

So, as outlined earlier with respect to our three steps of compassion—if someone is upset, acknowledge it. But Larry was very judgmental, and he found he couldn't accept why they were upset. Again, all he was doing was trying to manage a problem and not offer a way forward. He had to learn how to not judge.

So finally he started to grasp the wisdom of this approach. He asked for individual meetings with several of his workers and overtly affirmed that he understood how they felt. From the reports I had received they were surprised—I think "shocked" was the actual word that was used!

One of the problems plaguing his section was that two workers in particular appeared to act in tandem, taking advantage of corporate policies to call in sick together or otherwise strategizing how to miss as much work as possible. Of course that only incensed Larry. He'd been writing them up, and they really resented him. So he tried to inspire them with empathy and compassion, but they stayed away from him—not only were they suspicious of this new attitude but they wanted to continue with their shenanigans. Still, Larry continued to help his staff and made himself available to listen to their concerns and help them to solve their own work problems. After two weeks his people started to do better.

Now, at the time I'd first met Larry, his team already had the highest productivity in the company—of course some of this he was doing himself, he was taking on much more than his fair share. Nevertheless, their productivity rose even higher; and more notably, the complaints disappeared.

Now people were coming to Larry with ideas. They weren't hiding from him anymore, and he was finding himself with opportunities to teach rather than take over. His workers advanced their skills, which meant they took up more work and productivity increased.

Meanwhile, the two knucklehead guys were still doing their thing. Eventually, the group encountered a huge problem that required all hands on deck—everyone was needed to pitch in. Larry could never have handled such an emergency workload on his own—it was too much. And, as it turned out, everyone pitched in except these two guys. One called in sick, and the other showed up and said he wasn't capable enough to help. Then an interesting thing happened: the team members turned to this employee and suggested that he go home, that they'll take care of it. Larry didn't have to say anything.

This was the result of his genuine engagement with his staff—he dealt with the underlying issues by making personal connections. When the crisis came, if he had just been managing, that work would never been finished on time. This is the dark side of what happens when a manager fails to become a leader—everything goes south in an emergency. Instead, Larry achieved expanded productivity, expert crisis management, and ultimately a promotion. The only thing holding him back was his inability to delegate and the resentment that he was engendering. This is the victory of leadership over management.

As for the two guys who didn't want to work—they were let go. But no one questioned Larry about why. It was obvious. They knew that their leader gave these guys the opportunities, so they never held him responsible for their firings.

The bad seeds got separated out naturally. There was no need in the end to scold people in front of others. No one wanted them around anyway.

If the establishment of trust is the foundation of strong leadership, consistency is the key to maintaining it. We communicate more through actions than words. And again, citing Buddhist thought, actions to benefit others are not separate from actions that benefit ourselves. Words are easy; the integrity of acting upon your words will be what seals your reputation as a leader.

I remember working with an attorney in the entertainment business some time ago. She came in and won everyone over—she was very nice, capable, and attractive, possessing all of the superficial elements of what might appear to be a capable leader. The company was struggling, and I worked with her to help turn the company around. I started to observe early on though that she was establishing bonds of trust throughout the business but in the service of her own self-interest. What she was actually doing was maneuvering for position. And she was good at the game, so soon enough she secured herself a position of power to have the final say on most company business. She had ingratiated herself so expertly that she consolidated virtually all authority in her hands.

One day at a meeting one of the artists that the company catered to—basically one of its clients—brought up with me the nature of his new contract and referred to her as Miss Machiavelli. He then proceeded to tell me some about her lies, and her circulation of misinformation, and how she killed a deal for this struggling company in order to protect her own turf. Meanwhile the deal didn't get done—and that meant no one got paid. So she was willing to protect her fiefdom to the detriment of the company, and it didn't matter to her in the slightest who paid for that. Ultimately she became embroiled in a business scandal, improper transactions were discovered, and she was fired.

The success of a leader has little to do with fine words, classy speeches, motivational techniques, or downright charm.

Chapter 7

Getting Gold Out of Them

They Will Kill for You if You Demonstrate Real Concern

As we've learned, the main reason people work is ultimately to be acknowledged—money is not the primary motivation. A lot of people are shocked when they hear this, but it's absolutely true, and many studies have proven this to be so. David Rock and Jeffry Schwartz, in particular, demonstrate from a neuroscience perspective that this is a fact.[1] Money is useful as a means to attract or retain employees, but it doesn't influence behavior.

The building of meaningful relationships with your employees, based on care and consideration, is what matters most. Yet for many senior executives even acknowledging people can be a challenging thing to do. As a leader, you certainly need to understand yourself, but moreover you must come to understand the people working for you. What they want, most of all, is to trust you—they want stability and security. And they want you to be confident in the responsibilities you've entrusted them with. Millennial employees, in particular, will always respond to such challenges because they want to advance—they want a promotion, they want to make more money, and they want to be valued.

Millennial workers are already motivated to achieve because they were raised to seize opportunities to leave an impact, or an impression, on this world—or, more specifically, in their respective local environments or workplaces. Are your people happy? Are they satisfied? Do you even know the answers to these questions? If you don't, then you're not doing a good enough job as a leader. You have to be aware of your employees, and you need to initiate communications with them until you find out exactly what makes each of them tick. Just because a worker smiles when he or she sees you doesn't mean he or she is happy—your workers may just be doing that because that's what they think you want to see, and they're doing it to save their jobs.

So if it's not primarily the money they're paid, why do people love their jobs? Well, for one, happy workers are surrounded by people they like working with and for. It's your job, as a leader, to nurture such an environment. If you help to stimulate happiness and camaraderie among your reports, you will go a long way toward ensuring profitability, efficiency, and low turnover in your workplace.

Another important factor in workplace satisfaction is the freedom for workers to be creative, to improvise, and to not feel threatened if they make mistakes. Of course, you can't tolerate too many mistakes in a workplace, but there's a certain measure of autonomy that Millennials expect. Consider how to give them a long enough leash, so to speak, to express opinions, devise solutions, and be personally invested in the most meaningful company projects.

Millennials, of course, deeply value the quality of a company's business culture. This is more than offering free snacks and foosball tables—it's about creating a work environment that's transparent, with strong avenues of communication in both directions, trust, opportunities to be mentored, and an expectation that employees will be challenged. Millennials hate work environments that are a grind, or are mundane or repetitive.

Being tough on your reports isn't showing strength at all. Remarkably, a lot of managers still think that a lack of toughness is weakness, but that's a notion better left for the mid-20th century or earlier. Toughness reveals nothing but fear. Do you think your employee is less worthy or intelligent than you are because he or she is *only* a lower-level manager? Do you think a person's job title is in any way a measure of his or her inherent worth? Everyone has intrinsic value—Buddhists refer to this essential capacity as Buddhahood. In the words of the Buddhist philosopher Daisaku Ikeda, in "all matters there is a shallow and a profound perspective, including life itself. Do you live for yourself alone, or for a greater purpose and value? It is easy to live thinking only of oneself, but to live for a great ideal requires steadfast commitment and courage."

Don't underestimate your employees—if you do so, you're sowing the seeds for them to find another job, and that leaves you with the cost and necessity to fill that position again.

Why would anyone work hard for a boss who they know underestimates their abilities? How is shouting or toughness an incentive in such a case?

Instead, you have to reach out to your employees and demonstrate, in a sincere way, that you care about them, about their role in the company, and about their future successes. By doing so, you open the door to transparent communications. You can then speak to people directly without creating resentment. You can only be straightforward with a report if he or she knows, deep down, that you care about him or her. When your reports respect you, they even *want* to be treated in a direct and forthright manner. But if the relationship is predicated on resentment, they will only be defensive and unhappy. And they're probably already looking for another place to work.

A business leader isn't afraid to tell his or her reports what needs to be said—good or bad. The idea that toughness creates a vital distance, or a sense of authority or respect, is a delusion. Getting up close and personal with your employees does not preclude you from being tough on them when you need to be—in fact, it's the exact opposite.

It's a fallacy for managers to think that they don't need to focus on people because that takes them away from important work. That's just an excuse for managers not wanting to deal with others. Nobody wants to work for anyone who has this attitude—again, it breeds nothing but resentment. And in the long run, not focusing on people will create so many workplace problems that you won't even have time to concentrate on your work in any event. People are your most important resource! Not the job, not the salary, and not even the demands of your own boss. Caring for people is precisely the means to get your company to its successful end.

If you forestall conversations with others, you also cut yourself off from learning information they may have that might be very useful.

I started coaching someone named Maggie who was deemed a star at her company. She was very smart, had unique business experience, and had bagged many successful deals.

But Maggie was also in a very competitive, highly political, and male-dominated industry. She was in charge of a rapidly expanding department and wanted to focus on developing her leadership and management skills. One of the requirements of the job was to interact with the public. And because what she did was also so critical to the company's core business, she was obligated to present at large departmental meetings sometimes as well.

Although a talented hardcore businessperson, the one advantage Maggie had was that she genuinely cared about people. She came with this required component of successful leadership, which allowed me to work on her technique and skills. So one of the first things we focused on was how to acknowledge people. Maggie was so busy and devoted to her work that she rarely had the time to really think about if she was acknowledging enough the work of others. So when the next opportunity to present to one of the larger departments in the company came up, Maggie seized on the chance to present to this group in a different way. Instead of the usual offering up of numbers, results, and future goals, she started out by thanking the members of the group for their great work, and came right out and said she not only needed them, but she also really depended on them. Without them, she publicly acknowledged, she could not have achieved her goals and the company's goal.

The feedback from the group was, literally, that it was the best presentation they had ever experienced at the company.

To encourage optimum performance from people, you need to show them that you care.

It's essential to acknowledge what your workers and coworkers do, both good and bad—but here's an important caution: never reveal these aspects simultaneously. Interestingly, older people tend to only remember the negatives. Millennials, on the other hand, tend to retain only praise and at times dismiss constructive criticism.

Instead of criticizing, suggest ideas. Say let's solve this together. Win them over, get them to trust you, and then see them succeed. Nurture their self-respect. And if they don't have any, you've given them some by showing concern. If they feel cared for, and they have potential, they'll be inspired to work hard. This is where it's useful to do a SWOT analysis (a structured planning method used to evaluate the Strengths, Weaknesses, Opportunities, and Threats involved in a project or in a business venture) on your team as a whole, and the individual members of it.

The price of being a good leader is putting aside your concerns to focus on the other person. In turn, this allows you to get the results you need. If you don't do it, then you can't establish the open bond of trust to tell whether or not your reports are really performing to their best abilities.

I was very impressed once with the leadership of a CEO named Steve, who ran a rapidly growing small business. Steve asked me to coach one of the key managers in the company who had been working with him almost since its start. The company had doubled in size over a period of 18 months, and business was booming.

As with most businesses in a growth mode, responsibilities and pressure increases almost monthly, and this particular manager was working an unsustainable amount of hours. This is common; a manager is used to being responsible for a group of tasks. As the company grows, those tasks start to multiply, and the time to complete them decreases simultaneously. The manager, however, still tries to do all of the tasks as he or she did before. They're reluctant to delegate the work because they already know how to do it, and there's the chance that to whomever they delegate the task may screw it up.

There's a fine line, by the way, when you're developing your staff and growing successors between giving them responsibility so they take on more and expand their skill set, and giving them something that is too much for them to take on given their experience and skill set. A lazy manager will take on one thing, do it well, but then get piled up with too much stuff. You have to really know what a person's capabilities are and not just slide work from your plate to that person. If it's too much, what it all slides into is resentment. The person you're planning to train instead feels dumped on.

In the case of Steve's company, when coaxed to delegate some of the work to others, the manager would do so. However, if he noticed even the smallest issue with the work he would just take it back and do it himself. The result, of course, was that no one else learned how to do it, the manager remained overwhelmed, and eventually the work was late, done incorrectly, or both. The stress on this person got to the point where he was regularly staying at the office until midnight.

Steve asked me to coach this manager on how to delegate and take work off of his plate. He was also genuinely concerned about the manager's well-being, and he asked that I try to help coach him on taking better personal care of himself. The interesting part of this is that Steve actually was more concerned about the person than the job the person was doing. He obviously cared about him, but he also knew that he needed him to perform at his best in order to support the growth of the company. He instinctively realized that you can't have one without the other.

By the time I actually started working with the manager he was seriously beginning to crack under the pressure. The manager worked very hard to learn the techniques that would enable him to delegate effectively by planning in advance, creating critical paths for projects, teaching others how to do the work correctly, and finally learning how to leave them alone and not micromanage their work. His staff have since taken on new responsibilities, and they are performing well—without killing themselves.

The object of this story here is the attitude of the CEO. Steve was running a rapidly growing business under tremendous pressure. They had to hire new people weekly just to try and keep up with the demand, which added even more pressure because there really wasn't enough time to thoroughly vet every new hire. Steve himself was still closing deals and helping the less experienced managers learn the business. Yet despite all of that pressure he was compassionate enough and strategic enough to realize that he needed to help this person take care of himself for his own sake and for the sake of the company.

At times, of course, there will be communications problems, but these will be lessened if you maintain a pattern of consistent and regular conversations with those with whom you work. Consistency in this regard should be considered as a normal part of your job. It's a good idea to schedule periodic SWOTs with your employees to keep track of them, and to keep notes on their respective individual development. Tie what you learn to their career path objectives, and check back with them consistently. But be careful not to become complacent.

If you come to know your team well, and everyone is working together, there's a tendency to take things for granted. If team members are familiar with each other, some leaders start to back off of communications in order to devote themselves to other aspects of the work. This is a huge mistake, because all of your past hard work will start leaking out of your boat. Probably anyone who's been married will grasp this concept immediately! Don't let yourself get worn down—instead stay fresh, always motivated, and fired up.

You're the one who has to constantly refresh yourself as far as staying focused, leading your reports to where you want them to go. If you lose track, it'll appear as if you don't care—and you may have good reasons, such as work pressure, but this is where you have the opportunity to grow. Dig deep and do it.

How do some contemporary business leaders show concern toward their employees, and how does such concern result in profits? At Richard Branson's Virgin Group, for one, new mothers *and* fathers under certain circumstances can take off as much as a year with fully paid leave after the birth of a child. This isn't simply generous management, it's brilliant, foresighted leadership. Of course he's going to attract the best talent on Earth! People want to be devoted to their careers, but they also want to raise families. Virgin, with this move, appeals to the very best potential employees on the market who also desire to work in a culture that values time with their respective families. It attracts individuals with broad, well-balanced experience. And by demonstrating real concern for home life, Branson, in return, deepens the trust of his workers.

Other companies, such as Google, SAS, and Wegmans, are likewise highly regarded for the care and consideration they shower on their employees—it's no wonder each of these consistently ranks among the top corporations people want to work for. Google, of course, is perhaps the American gold standard with respect to demonstrating the sort of strategic compassion that makes for a successful company. Employees there rave about the camaraderie they enjoy at the office, not to mention the free food that's provided and the challenge and pride of working on cutting-edge technologies. Workers at SAS Institute enjoy artists in residence, a swimming pool, programs to support child and elder care, and other incentives that promote work-life balance. And at Wegmans, a supermarket chain, employees benefit from generous tuition support incentives, fully funded healthcare insurance programs, and a caring culture that includes flexible hours and exercise opportunities. Clearly the leaders of each of these corporations understand what's their most important business commodity—their employees. Who in their right mind would ever want to leave?

How else do business leaders, on a more mundane, day-to-day level engender the trust and devotion of their workers? For one thing, if someone is being attacked, people will never forget those who stand beside them and show conspicuous support. Think about—in fact, write down a time when someone did this for you. How did it feel for you when a person supported you in a bad spot? How did it feel to have a mentor looking out for you whether it was for his or her immediate benefit or not? Would you ever forget this episode in your life?

Excellent leadership really comes down to consistency in using the tools of strategic compassion, open communications, and care. People respond far better when they feel respected.

Most corporate executives will admit that the hardest aspect of their businesses is identifying and hiring the right people. In a 2014 CNBC report, fully 77 percent of corporations surveyed reported that new hires straight out of college don't last even as long as a year at their firms. And a recent survey from the Conference Board determined that more than 50 percent of employees are unhappy at work. It is so much more efficient to care for the workers that you have as compared to finding new ones who have to be identified, trained—and nurtured just as sure as the old ones did.

Onboarding a new member to your team means to be inclusive. One of the key things to consider is that many times your more established staff may be nervous. And sometimes people will try to intimidate the new hire.

When you see new hires coming to the team, one of the things that happens sometimes is that they don't want to look like a fool and not appear they don't know what's going on. So they don't ask questions. That contributes to a negative company culture. Make sure when someone new comes on board, in a meeting, you take the time in front of the team to explain to them what's going on, how we work, and how we behave. Don't throw around words or terms or acronyms they're not familiar with. You want them to feel secure.

I worked recently with a young guy named Kevin—a brilliant executive, who was only 26 years old and off the charts smart. He had a very calm demeanor, he generally cared about other people, he rarely got upset, and he possessed all of the critical leadership traits. Suddenly he was put in charge of a project that was vital to the company's CEO replacing a much older director who had been fired for failing to accomplish the CEO's goal. And it was not a promotion—rather, he slotted in there without full title and pay to see if he can pull it off. In other words, let's see if you can do it, and then we'll decide whether you're up to the task.

Now this Millennial executive had a team to run, which he'd never done before. I will say this—he wrote down everything I said to him, he questioned everything, he was an expert student. And he tried to implement the notion of strategic compassion right away. His staff, as well, were all Millennial age, so at first they were excited not to have the old boss around. But of course there was also resentment, which is natural for any generation because they were all the same age. And then Kevin had to let some people go.

To make matters worse, a lot of heat was piled on him at the director-level departmental meetings. The CEO put direct heat on him during these gatherings. So he was regularly in the line of yelling, screaming, pushback, and generally right on the edge of folding due to the pressure. He was beginning to feel disheartened, as if there wasn't answer to the problem—that there was, in his mind, no way to accomplish such an impossible task.

I suggested that he tell his immediate supervisor exactly how he felt. So he did. And at the next three meetings the same thing happened. But now this particular boss stood up for him. He said that a plan was in place, give us time, we'll keep you posted. The boss publicly had his back. This took the heat off of Kevin and, with this support, he had the liberty to take chances with his reports. It was a baptism by fire but they took the risk and got the job done.

The executive stood between the CEO and the kid. The executive, at significant personal risk, took the chance on protecting Kevin, and that enabled the younger man to come through. It never would have worked if he had to fight the CEO directly. That's the wisdom of a boss who acts as a leader—he stood in the line of fire to protect the company's greater goals. And by doing that he got the best out of Kevin and his team. That's a guy with experience. Now everyone wants to work for this executive.

When you give your workers self-respect and pride, they perform far better. There's no raise or promotion involved, there's no money directly at stake. And more money wouldn't have worked anyway—would Kevin had performed any better with a sack of cash on his desk? Absolutely not. What he needed, and what his immediate boss delivered, was the intangible quality of leadership. This, for more than financial incentive, is the most meaningful tool available to get the most out of people with whom you work.

Imagine two people, and they're both building a house on a hill in Southern California. It's very nice out there, with lots of Pacific Ocean views and terrific weather, but there are also earthquakes and floods and mudslides. Let's say you're very well aware of what changes *might* come in the future, so you sacrifice a thousand square feet off of your structure to build a deep foundation into the ground. Your neighbor builds too, but he likes that extra thousand square feet, so he forgoes the stronger-than-necessary foundation. His house looks nice—nicer and larger than yours in fact. In the meantime, you just sank $200,000 to install caissons that no one will ever see in an effort to be sure your house is safe.

When the earthquake hits, your house has broken glass. His house, unfortunately, is destroyed. Your roots were deeper, and that's the proper way to build.

In business, I'm suggesting that you ought to invest in something that's not flashy and not even visible at times because you want to be as sure as possible that your house remains standing. If you adopt the three steps to compassion, learn how to manage your emotional triggers, implement the principles of strategic compassion, then you'll have a set of business chops that almost no other people possess.

NOTE

1. See, e.g., Tara Swart, Kitty Chisholm, and Paul Brown, *The Neuroscience of Leadership: Harnessing the Brain Gain Advantage* (New York: Palgrave Macmillan, 2015).

Chapter 8

Dealing with Pushback

The Art of War in Contemporary Business

Millennials won't necessarily believe you and your humanistic approach right away. They won't believe you're sincere because they're used to working for jerks. Leaders understand that they have to work hard to win the trust of their workers, because they won't get it overnight. People won't necessarily respond as you expect—and this is where many people will be swayed or give up. Of course, you can't expect people to just trust you right away if you've only recently changed your behavior, or if you're newly appointed to a management position.

So how do you deal with coworkers who undermine you and sabotage the workplace? Approach them directly, praise them to the extent they have any worthy ideas, and then tell them you have a better way of doing it. If they expect you to punch, don't punch. Control your emotional triggers. If they say they don't believe in strategic compassion, ask why. Ask if they have a better way. Let them think you're vulnerable—that's exactly where you want them to be.

Of course, you'll also need to be supported politically, so tell your supervisors what you're doing from the standpoint of how it supports them. Is your humanistic approach helping the company's stakeholders to get to where they want to go? Work to involve your boss so that he's or she invested in the success of your team. As was the case with Larry at the machine shop, when employees try to undermine you they will stick out, and their behavior will not be acceptable to their peers. But you've got to be patient. Separate out the bad egg, and work around him or her with everyone else. Then the problem worker will be standing there all by himself or herself. There's no need to drive a knife into anyone—always avoid the triggers that drop you into an angry or animalistic response.

It is no secret, of course, that contemporary business is viewed in general as warfare. Here's a popular example—consider this take on how to do business from Kevin O'Leary, the billionaire originator of the Learning Channel: "My attitude is business is war. You send out your soldiers every day in the form of your capital, and you want them to come home with prisoners. You want to salt the earth that your competitor is lurking on. You want to steal their market share. You want to destroy them and get their customers."[1] And who's to argue with a self-made billionaire?

But take note—nowhere in O'Leary's comment is the suggestion that such aggressive tactics ought to be directed toward your *own* company and staff. So go out and crush the competition, but certainly don't behave like that toward your own team.

This notion that business is war has its philosophical roots in the 16th-century work known as *The Prince*, by Niccolo Machiavelli. Many of us read it perhaps in high school. Machiavelli considered power and the nature of sovereignty, or in his day public leadership, through the eyes of a rational scientist. His work is famous for focusing on achieving the goal without regards for morals and ethics. His worldview is more about the tactics of retaining power, really, than it is about contemporary capitalism, but many executives today still rely on Machiavelli's vision, at least unconsciously, to expand and grow their businesses.

In describing the qualities of a good leader, Machiavelli holds that he or she should be feared rather than loved, if one can't be both; have the support of his people; be virtuous; and be intelligent. It's the first element here that has particularly trickled down to saturate our contemporary business mores—and the one that strategic compassion seeks to stamp out.

The earlier example of Johnson & Johnson notwithstanding, successful corporations obviously don't exist per se for the good of their employees or the general good of their communities. Many companies continue to be profitable while polluting the environment. Other companies market dangerous products, and still more will rely on deceit—or, let's say, *ahem*, heavy marketing—to boost their bottom lines.

Modern business thinkers will point to Machiavelli's apparent approval of fraud or treachery as acceptable tactics; his cold-eyed view that a lesser evil can be considered as a good; and his suggestion that leaders aren't required to keep promises when it's no longer advantageous for them to do so. For these reasons, his name has become an adjective for describing someone in business who's devious, deceitful, and self-serving (i.e., "Machiavellian").

At the end of the day, Machiavelli, for all his five centuries of repute and notoriety, didn't care to create value; his approach, instead, was about destruction. The context of how to do business today is different from what it was in 16th-century Europe. Where lines of responsibility aren't clear, perhaps maneuvering might work, but people who maneuver as a matter of course eventually will be exposed by the truth of their self-serving actions. And when the time is right, they're called out about what they've done—their machinations, almost always, are ultimately revealed.

More to the point, it's one thing to be Machiavellian toward the competition but quite another to conduct yourself inside of a company as if your colleagues are the enemy. It amazes me, nevertheless, how many managers fail to distinguish between the two. Even Machiavelli himself never suggested to resort to fraud or treachery against those who are on your side!

So if someone pushes back against your new way of doing things, which he or she often will, don't engage. Remember your emotional triggers and control your reactions. What creates more value—indulging the emotion that gets you angry, or withholding from engagement in a long, drawn-out battle because your rational judgment knows its preferable to not waste the company's time or money? When you react in defense against someone pushing back, you're wasting resources—always. Machiavellian politics in business and posing as the tough guy can take your eye off of the ball. All you're doing at this point is trying to keep the car on the road instead of moving forward.

Dealing with pushback requires guts. You have to stand alone, hold the course, and outlast whatever the bad behavior is. You're the last person standing. This requires control, patience, and the mastering of your emotional triggers. To succeed in anything, you have to be stronger than the pushback—on the inside. And if you read Machiavelli at all, read him in this light: if business is war, then make sure you're armed to the teeth in self-respect, control, farsightedness, and confidence.

In contrast to Machiavelli's foundational roots from which the concepts of contemporary business appear to spring, the idea of strategic compassion outlined here is loosely based, as referenced throughout, on a Buddhist perspective toward life. How does a Buddhist stay unshakable? How does a Buddhist maintain control over his or her emotional triggers?

A helpful method toward understanding, from an introductory perspective, how Buddhism views the conditions of life was developed by the sixth-century Buddhist monk and Lotus Sutra scholar Zhiyi, also known as T'ien-T'ai. He viewed the human experience through the perspective of "Ten Worlds." These worlds, from highest to lowest, are:

- BUDDHAHOOD: Enlightenment—a condition of life free from delusion and fear.
- BODHISATTVA: A condition of life filled with compassion for others.
- REALIZATION: The inherent ability to perceive the true nature of phenomena.
- LEARNING: A condition of life in which one aspires to enlightenment.
- RAPTURE: A state of life experienced when desires are fulfilled.
- TRANQUILITY: A peaceful state of life characterized by the ability to reason.
- ANGER: A state of life consumed by the need to dominate others—often accompanied by a pretense of being good or wise.
- ANIMALITY: An instinctual state of life characterized by fearing the strong and bullying the weak.
- HUNGER: A state of life governed by deluded cravings or desires that are impossible to fulfill.
- HELL: A condition of seemingly powerless despair, in which one is trapped in overwhelming suffering.

The idea is that each person has a predominant state of life corresponding to one of these worlds. But these aren't fixed conditions—people throughout their lives will migrate up or down the scale. Especially those of us in the rough and tumble world of business might tend to cycle between the lower few worlds, with the occasional glimpses of Rapture.

Still, this concept is an optimistic view of life. It suggests that people are not inevitably swayed by their environments; rather they have control over the vicissitudes of life—or, in our case, business. The Japanese Buddhist monk, Nichiren Daishonin, pointed to this control stating that each individual has over the things that appear to happen to him or her: "To illustrate, environment is like the shadow, and life, the body. Without the body, no shadow can exist, and without life, no environment." To be sure, it is the individual, and not the intensity of events happening around him, that determines the ultimate outcome and propels the means to triumph.

If you think about it, this strength, that some people possess in good measure but rare leaders possess in quantity, must be the stuff that makes a good businessperson great. How else does an innovator withstand the avalanche of criticism launched his or her way by the disbelievers and naysayers who are always there to block his or her paths? And they are always there—no one ever accomplished something great easily. Inevitably one will have to overcome tremendous obstacles to achieve greatness.

When everyone is freaking out, the one who stays cool and focused is the true leader. He or she is the one to lead the way out of crisis. In this kind of a situation many times a person appears who no one ever expected to have leadership abilities. And the person who's supposed to be in charge shrinks. It's in a crisis when a leader can emerge for everyone to see. Who among the affected group will step up to find a way forward?

I always thought Gene Kranz, the former NASA Flight director during the Apollo 13 drama, is a terrific example of someone who possesses unshakable cool under fire. He was played by Ed Harris in the film *Apollo 13*, and he became famous for the comment, "failure is not an option." Kranz and his team were on duty when part of the Apollo 13 service module exploded during its mission, and they were responsible for handling the potentially deadly crisis. They calculated and later set the constraints for the consumption of spacecraft consumables, including oxygen and water, and controlled the three-course correction burns during the trans-Earth trajectory, as well as the power-up procedures that brought the astronauts back to Earth in the command module. Throughout, Kranz stayed preternaturally calm and kept his team heading in the right direction. He appeared solid as a rock during the crisis, because he was indeed solid as a rock on the inside as well. Another more recent aviation-related individual, Chesley Sullenberger, who in 2009 landed his failing commercial US Airways flight in the middle of the Hudson River, is hailed for his similar abilities to function well in crisis.

In the business world, a well-recognized contemporary example of strong-willed leadership is Elon Musk. Musk is a far-sighted pacesetter and among the world's top business innovators. He's the founder and CEO of Space Exploration Technologies (SpaceX), CEO and product architect of Tesla Motors, and chairman of SolarCity. He's also a cofounder of Paypal, among other companies. Musk founded SpaceX in 2002 with the goal of no less creating technologies to enable humanity to reduce space transportation costs and enable the sustainable colonization of Mars with fully and rapidly reusable rockets. The company's successful technology is already exceeding Musk's own brutally ambitious schedule. Tesla Motors, for its part, designs, manufactures, and sells electric cars, electric vehicle powertrain components, and battery products. It produced the Tesla Roadster, the first fully electric sports car, which as of 2016 runs approximately 250 miles on a charge and goes 0–60 mph in 3.7 seconds, and today produces the incredible Tesla Model sedan. Since 2008, Tesla has delivered about 70,000 electric cars to consumers. The then-vice chairman of General Motors said in 2009—when Musk's company was still far from a sure thing—that "[a]ll the geniuses here at General Motors kept saying lithium-ion technology is ten years away, and Toyota agreed with us—and boom, along comes Tesla. So I said, 'How come some tiny little California startup, run by guys who know nothing about the car business, can do this, and we can't?'" Tesla is on track to deliver an electric car to consumers priced at about $35,000 in 2017. If you haven't noticed yet, the next wave of car industry innovations has already begun.

Clearly Musk is an engineering and business genius—he started his first company with $28,000 of borrowed money and flipped it four years later for $22 million; he then co-developed and rebranded a small online money transfer he called Paypal, which was sold three years later to eBay with Musk pocketing $165 million from the transaction. But intelligence aside, Musk also is keenly aware about how to not only surround himself with smart, hard-working colleagues but he also empowers them to commit themselves to a deep-seated shared corporate vision. There were times when Tesla looked like it would fail. A guy like this is simply not swayed.

So if shouting at people and attempting to motivate them through fear is a bankrupt strategy, how does a business leader build the sort of inner strength to see the way through a strategically compassionate breakthrough? Is it a mysterious quality that people either have or don't? Is it something that can be acquired through training—like muscles are built by lifting weights?

Of course, everyone is born with the capacity for great inner strength, but, like many other things, not everyone has the knowledge about how to develop it. It's like any other skill—you need determination and at least a measure of some tough, self-discipline.

For one, the ability to manage and to refrain from wasting time with unnecessary workplace activities—and the developing strength to master your own emotional triggers—will build your inner strength. And, as with weightlifting, you get stronger the more you exercise these particular abilities.

Inner strength is the only true defense available to you when you face pushback at the workplace. Sure, you can play politics all you want and attempt to outmaneuver your adversary, but then you're on his or her ground—and, to cite another ancient text often relied on by contemporary business consultants, *The Art of War*, by Sun Tzu, it's far more preferable to fight your battles on your ground. Let your adversary come to you. And what's the most advantageous arena for a leader who practices strategic compassion in the workplace? Clearly, the one in which inner strength allows you to control your emotions while your adversary, so to speak, is stuck in the world of anger.

Strength is gained by the person who uses his or her inner capacity to develop the resources needed to withstand difficulties and obstacles. Inner strength provides energy and stamina—more so than your adversary who almost certainly attacks you from an emotional condition of life. Individuals who throw obstacles in the way of a good leader are uniformly acting out of their own self-interests. They're upset not because they disagree inherently with your ideas or approach, but because they feel threatened in some way—either their authority has been diminished or their job may be perceived to be at risk—and so they will be vicious at times to try to stop you. But again, if you withstand the attacks, and conduct yourself with dignity, two things will happen.

First, they will almost always burn out before you do, and you will outlast their assault. Second, you will undoubtedly gain the respect of your peers, and they'll stand out in a light that portrays them as emotional, shortsighted, or inconsiderate.

The truth is that the inner strength I'm observing is the polar opposite of aggression. Machiavelli is about pure aggression; strategic compassion turns that on its head—it promises success in business largely through self-control and inner strength. Millennials are calibrated to appreciate this distinction. More than anything we're judged based on our actions, and when Millennials see someone lose his or her cool, it becomes very difficult, or even near impossible, to reverse that negative impression.

Managers who shout and departmental directors who are aggressive are actually insecure. Know this about them when you see it—it's the honest truth. They need to use loud voices, and even violent expressions, as a means to cover for their lack of inner strength—that's exactly what a bully does. Strong people, on the other hand, can stay cool because they know they're going to get to the bottom of what the underlying conflict is. Insecure people don't want to do that—that's the last place they would want to be! In the words of the Dalai Lama, "A person who practices compassion and forgiveness has greater inner strength, whereas aggression is usually a sign of weakness." Strong individuals who know they have the tools, power, and skills to resolve a situation have no need whatsoever to act aggressively.

A man I know and respect, Don, was the CFO of a major manufacturing company during the economic downturn in 2008. The company's revenues plummeted, and they had decided to lay off more than 1,000 people. The CEO and the COO both quit the company and took their parachutes before all of this was to occur. The board then left Don with the unenviable task of figuring out how to cut costs and keep the company afloat until things turned around.

Don came up with two different scenarios to cut costs. The first one was to package out most of the employees and give them a severance that would have lasted them maybe a month or so. The second was to drastically cut their salaries but have them keep their jobs, in hopes that the company would turn around.

Don had had many arguments with his board of directors over the years, and he had always taken the side of the employees when there was a conflict. He was very good at his job, however, and the board didn't want to lose him, so they would basically always put up with his going against them and come up with a compromise.

This time was different. The company stock was tanking, and they were demanding severe cuts right away—the CEO and COO, who ran as soon as things got really uncomfortable, had damaged the company worse than anyone knew. To top it off, part of the company was unionized, and now the union was threatening to sue if the reduction in pay plan was implemented.

I spoke to Don about the problem and the turmoil he was experiencing. He knew a lot of the employees and their families. He knew exactly that the direct layoff would result in people possibly losing their homes and having to take their kids out of college. He was also well aware that the job market was the worst it had been in 40 years and that the chance of them finding jobs once they were laid off was remote at best. The only solution that would give people a fighting chance was to reduce their pay, keep the doors open, and let them keep their jobs in the hope that the economy would turn around sooner than later, and that then, as soon as he could, he would be able to get their pay back up and make the company profitable.

Don was a passionate guy, and he had on occasion blown up in board meetings, and in meetings with the union before. He had worked very hard on putting together the salary reduction plan and wanted to get it approved by the board and the union quickly.

He was already furious with whom he considered the greedier members of the board and one of the union leaders trying to make a name for himself. We talked about this before the big meeting between all the parties.

Don knew well that he would react hotly to any pushback; we discussed that trigger and how to control it. He agreed to give it a try because he was about to play his last card—he's either get this plan approved or face the layoffs. One of the board members was an investment banker, and Don found him to be especially avaricious. This guy reminded him of a banker that had foreclosed on his best friend's home when he was a kid. He remembered the pain it caused his friend and his family. Whenever he saw this board member, he would think about that banker from years ago, and go right at the guy in meetings.

But this time would be different. Don controlled his temper, and when the banker started screaming at Don about how his plan "sucked," Don quietly sat there and looked the guy in the eye. When the banker was finished, Don simply said that he understood this man's concerns but the alternative was for the company to lose even more money when the economy turned around, at which time the company wouldn't have the manpower to compete against its rivals. And that would mean the end of the business.

The room fell silent, and Don went through all the details of his plan with them. They approved it, and the banker looked like a fool for being the only board member to rant and rave like an angry child. When Don met with the union, he spoke directly to the union leader who was trying to make a name for himself by getting Don's plan rejected. He went through all of the union's concerns before the representative even spoke. Instead of upsetting the union rep, and falling prey to his own justified anger as well, Don calmly but completely disarmed the guy and his argument. The union, like the board of the directors, approved the plan.

All ended happily—just as Don had predicted, when the economy turned around the company had the necessary labor to take on the increased product demand. He was able to get everyone's pay almost back to where it was before. The workers, naturally, had great appreciation for what Don had done for them. The company actually gained market share, as some of their competitors had themselves laid off too many workers and couldn't hire fast enough to keep up with the now-increased pace of business.

Don had stood up in the face of extreme pressure, and he kept his cool. He was the only executive to devise a rational, logical plan in the midst of chaos. He also was the only one who had the courage to take on the challenge and not run to take what he could get, like the CEO and COO had done. Most of all, Don had overcome his anger and resentment toward the investment banker and the union leader, both of whom could have derailed the entire plan.

One final note: Don retired in 2013, and on the last day when he left the office, more than 500 employees lined up cheering and clapping for Don to show how much they really appreciated him. If he hadn't marshaled his inner strength, he would never have experienced this ultimate triumph.

Don knew, right from the beginning, that he'd be strong enough to see it through—but he had to stand alone at the time. It wasn't until much later that others began to appreciate what he actually had accomplished.

When a person lifts weights, it's easy to see that he has gained muscle. Likewise, when someone starts to train and watch what he or she eats, the loss of weight becomes clearly evident. It's a lot harder to notice changes in inner strength, however. You may know that you've changed—and you may have even changed a lot in a short team—but the people with whom you work still expect the old you. They may not reflect quite so quickly the changes that you've been seeking to impart.

They will notice a few things, however. Perhaps you shout less or appear to be happier at the office? Are you in a better mood? Are more people coming to you to ask for advice? Are you more optimistic or relaxed? Most importantly, is your department functioning more efficiently, and is profitability on the rise? These are likely symptoms of your inner changes. And as Buddhism illustrates, it's the shadow, or the environment, that bends with the body—not the other way around.

Another way to breakdown the process of managing emotional triggers is to see the way you negotiate your interactions through three factors: the challenges you face, the vulnerabilities these challenges agitate, and the strengths you have to meet those challenges.

If you stay attached to the long-term sensitivities that form your emotional triggers, your identity starts to be shaped around them. If you've always been sensitive, anxious, and shy, for example, well then you might as well decide that that's just the way you are. But if you manage the stimuli that cause, for example, a certain nervousness associated with anxiety that may be holding you back in the workplace, then your self-image and self-conditioning will change—just as the shadow follows the body.

I'm not trying to encourage anyone in a psychological context, but rather I'm making the point that in business any person is capable of improving himself or herself. And to be successful in business you'd be a lot better off organizing yourself not around anger, anxiety, and fear but instead around strength, resilience, and compassion. In other words, you need to deliberately compel yourself to do so. In the workplace, inner strength defeats the appearance of outer strength every time.

There are a lot of ways to build inner strength, of course, and these range from belief in yourself, to the setting of reasonable goals, the studies and practices of religious philosophies and meditation, or the engagement in sports training and other physical practices that demand mental toughness. In whatever it is you do, however, it will take intention, effort, and courage to see it through.

At the end of the day, though, the fastest way to strengthen your inner resolve is to confront difficult situations—one after another after another. Nothing can make you grow faster than adversity. And in this, small steps are key—don't expect to change overnight. As Aristotle wrote some 2,000 years ago, "We are what we repeatedly do. Excellence then, is not an act, but a habit."

NOTE

1. Richard Feloni, "*Shark Tank* investor Kevin O'Leary explains why 'business is war,'" *Business Insider* (February 5, 2015), available at http://www.businessinsider.com/shark-tank-investor-kevin-oleary-2015-2

Chapter 9

How to Lead Meetings

Never Engage without a Plan

The art of running an efficient and productive meeting is one of the most underappreciated aspects of business leadership. It's true that in reality a vast majority of Millennials in business loathe going to meetings (just like the rest of us). They're often boring, unfocused, and conclude without reaching solutions, leaving exiting participants whispering to each other under their breath: "well, that was a waste of time."

As a general rule, have meetings when you need them. If you already know what the decision at hand should be, then ask yourself whether you even need the meeting. If that's the case, you will certainly want to communicate the decision, but that may not require a discussion. Let's be real—blowhards love meetings; too many people show up for the coffee and junk food or to prognosticate about what everyone already knows. It's up to you, though, as the leader to control this, and to get people to think and be prepared.

Another problem with poorly run meetings is that they just run on and on—meetings can kill you. You have to be specific about what you want out of a meeting, get it done and get out. If not, then people will not want to come to your meetings. And, you as a leader or manager will do anything to avoid them because such wide-ranging discussions will feel out of control, and it seems that nothing ever gets done. Such meetings are wildly inefficient, depriving entire departments from otherwise productive work hours.

On the other hand, if you decide that it's beneficial to meet, a properly run meeting can provide a host of information. Through an efficient meeting, or over a series of regular, weekly meetings, not only could the business at hand be resolved, but also productivity could improve, relations between coworkers could be enhanced, untapped talent is likely to emerge, and the head of the meeting ideally can establish his or her authority to lead a successful and profitable department.

How do you best manage a meeting, and specifically how do you use group meetings to get the most out of your staff? The first point to recognize is that meetings are precious opportunities to build confidence with your team. You control the meeting—that's why these are critical moments to exercise leadership. You have to make sure everyone contributes, which you do by nurturing an environment where everyone is comfortable speaking. Engage everyone.

Here are the essential steps to running a successful meeting:

1. Before you call the meeting, set the goal—be clear about what you want to accomplish, and write it down.
2. Determine exactly who needs to be in the specific meeting to contribute to the end goal.
3. Alert the people who need to be in the meeting what you want them to bring to the meeting.
4. Determine what you're going to say at the top of the meeting. Start the meeting by thanking them, and state what you're meeting about and what you want to accomplish. Then let them know that everyone will have a chance to speak, and then follow that up with open discussion at the end of the meeting. State how long the meeting will take, and stick to it. Then do simple math—divide the number of people in the meeting and delegate the time accordingly; figure this out before you start the meeting. If you've got an hour and 10 people are in the meeting, for example, you might allot 5 minutes/speaker, and then 10 minutes for discussion. Make sure everyone is clear that they'll have their chance, and how long they'll have to present their thoughts.
5. If someone interrupts the speaker who has the floor, jump in and say good point—we'll discuss it at the end. But first, let's let her finish and give the floor right back to the speaker. A few things are accomplished in this way: first, everyone knows they have to contribute, so they had better prepare something; and second, you're reconfirming that no one will be interrupted. That it will not be tolerated, and you're going to be stopped if you interrupt. You've accomplished three goals toward leading a successful meeting right there.

The secret ingredient to the management of a successful meeting is related to how you manage yourself at the meeting—in particular, how do you train yourself to listen? Let everyone speak first. Keep in mind because meetings can have different agendas and participants, there should be no predetermined notion of what a meeting should look like. The point is how to run a logical and productive dialogue, and how to provide a platform for others.

A couple of years ago I was brought into coach the senior vice president (SVP) of sales for a large tech firm. Jack was a great guy and definitely had the backslapping, smiling sales approach down pat—he was charming and relentless at the same time, and his success in sales proved that.

Jack had been recently promoted to the SVP role as a result of the revenue he'd brought in individually and as a national sales team manager. Now that he was promoted, his new role required him to lead meetings with senior executives at corporate headquarters. This was very different from the virtual meetings he had previously led with his national sales team.

Jack was failing badly at running the corporate meetings. He would commandeer the gatherings and argue his point before listening to the opinions of the other senior executives in the room. They were more senior than Jack and far more experienced in handling corporate issues. His lack of experience at this higher level was obvious to them, and while they supported his promotion they were getting concerned that if he didn't change his style he'd lose that support. It could have even led to his dismissal. By the time I started coaching Jack he was afraid and bewildered because of the reaction to his leadership style. Everything he had done before worked, his style had increased the company's revenues substantially. So why wasn't it working now?

I listened in on one of Jack's sales meetings. He exhibited a typical authoritative style, where Jack dominated the speaking time, giving directions and goals, and then asking questions about the deals his people had negotiated. Jack also possessed an annoying tendency of some sales people to just keep pushing with one argument after another without listening or responding to other team members. Some of his arguments were emotional and didn't make a whole lot of sense. So we started working on what he had to do to be more successful.

I asked Jack how much he would study the agenda and content of a meeting before he went into it. He told me he made up the agenda and that was it. He didn't study much at all about the content, because he knew what the company sold as well as he knew the back of his hand. He felt as if he didn't have to look into it any further.

That's the first thing we corrected. I told him that he needed to start studying the night before the meeting and completely understand what the corporate issues were, not just what the company was selling. Jack resisted at first, he was used to going out to dinner and drinks with clients and the local staff—how could he do both?

Going out to dinner with clients is what had helped him to get the promotion, but now he had to let the new vice president of sales do that. Unless he really knew all he had to know to successfully run a senior management meeting, he knew deep down that not only his promotion, but his job too, was in jeopardy.

I suggested to him that a promotion is something you earn *after* you get it. Now he had to learn, study, and understand more about the company as he moved up the ladder. For example, he should know what the concerns were of each person in the meeting beforehand—otherwise, how could he respond to them in a cogent way and add value to the meeting? He wasn't just going to get away with bulldozing and glad-handing executives at this level. I was pretty tough on him, because he had that hard sales veteran shell on him and it wasn't easy to crack through it, but eventually he got it. I then took him through the steps to leading a meeting, particularly allowing everyone to speak before he did. I compelled him to come up with an end goal for each meeting and consult with all of the other senior executives beforehand to find out what they wanted to contribute to the meeting.

I also told him it might be a good idea to take each of them to lunch and really get to know them and what their concerns were. We then went through some of his triggers and how to manage them. One was that as soon as he spoke to the group about a particular point and they didn't nod in agreement he'd right away continue to sell it, instead of listening to what they had to say about it. This of course would aggravate everyone, as well as disrespect them—from their perspective, it was as if their point didn't matter. Jack's training to close a deal was so deeply ingrained that he had to fight the tendency to keep selling in these meetings. However, once he had taken each of the senior managers to lunch, he learned that he could relax in front of them, that they were not just there to say no, and conversely he wasn't there just to get them to say yes! Rather, he was there to help the group resolve issues and determine future product development and the strategy to sell it. (Again homework, and research, which he'd never done before.)

Within a month, after four meetings, Jack had won over every one of the other senior managers. He still had the remarkable charm, and that certainly helped. But he ran the meetings as we had discussed, and other executives commented on the maturity and growth they saw in him. Also the research he did, and his newfound ability to listen to other managers, gave Jack a knowledge base on his industry that he didn't have before.

Consequently, he started contributing ideas that he had never thought of before because he simply didn't have this knowledge before.

The ability to rely on charm, or humor, or at least to tell a good story, goes a long way. Lots of managers and executives are bombarded with data and analytics. How do you get people to understand what's behind the numbers? Excellent storytelling resonates on both an intellectual and emotional level. The very best leaders synthesize the relevant information and present it in a clear and entertaining manner in order for coworkers to quickly grasp even the most complex concepts. You've got to discern the capacity of any given group, and adjust your ability to conduct the meeting accordingly.

Think about your experiences in departmental meetings. When they're not led well, people are interrupting others, it's a free for all—in these sorts of gatherings, what are you most concerned about? For most people, it's about wondering when you're going to get your chance to share your ideas. But then, you're also not listening to what other people are saying—you're just waiting for your shot. And everyone else in that meeting is waiting for his and hers.

There are always shy, and quiet people. But they're important parts of the team. In a badly run meeting a shy person will feel intimidated and not speak up, and consequently you may lose a great idea—shy people actually are often quite thoughtful. If they don't have a chance to communicate, or they're afraid they'll be put down if they do, you lose what they can contribute, which of course could be the solution or idea you are desperately looking for.

A young, Millennial executive I knew named Jake took over a group from an older guy who had been asked to leave a media company. The group had a troubled history and a poor reputation within the company for lack of productivity and general inefficiency. There was a lot of divisiveness within the department—a couple of older executives had been there for years, while most of the other 15 or so people who comprised the department were younger Millennials. They had longstanding weekly meetings set for each Monday.

Jake, being a new guy but an executive considered to have significant potential, had only managed deals before—now he had people to manage. So he walks in, and a couple of the older group members by nature already didn't respect him because they thought one of them should have been promoted to the position. Naturally Jake felt he had to be strong and decisive to lead—he wanted to show the group that he was in charge, and he felt he had to prove himself. So Jake would set forth in the meeting the targets for the week, and he delegated who was responsible for which priorities.

Right away, one of the older reports interrupted him to challenge what the priority actually should be. So Jake responded forcefully, and proceeded to get himself into an argument. Then another older employee piped up, challenging what either of them thought should have been prioritized. The meeting quickly unraveled.

This occurred week after week, and Jake was becoming more and more of a dictator. During this whole time, they were undermining Jake, and so Jake felt as if he had to solidify even further the false persona of a tough guy. Meanwhile, nothing was getting done at the meetings. Finally, the older guys just started to clam up. In fact, even worse, they would whisper to themselves while Jake tried to address the group, showing complete disrespect. The younger Millennials, of course, didn't say anything either, because they observed Jake always hammering whomever was in disagreement—it didn't look safe for them to speak up. Ultimately, no one felt safe enough to offer any thoughts to the discussion. Each Monday morning, Jake was just lecturing these 15 people.

So by the time we met, Jake was seething about the older guys disrespecting and badmouthing him and was thinking of canceling the weekly meeting. Yet the forum to really start leading this group was ideally this meeting—the entire team was there. The challenge for Jake was that they would all, of course, follow his behavior—and not necessarily listen to what he was saying.

We started working on emotional triggers and developing an understanding of where the older guys were coming from. When they spoke up at the meeting, as they inevitably would, I encouraged Jake to acknowledge that they may have a good point, but ask that they all could consider it later on. That stops them from interfering, and it enables Jake to continue—that's much more effective than arguing with them during the meeting and intimidating others. Second, Jake needed to seriously clarify the actual goal for the meeting, and to make it simple. Don't come in with three or four agenda items and leave with no resolution—come in with one or two and get something done. So before the next meeting was held, he implemented these steps toward the one most important goal they had as a group, and he assigned everyone a set time to speak.

Right away at this next meeting, one of the older guys raised all the other issues that weren't on the agenda. Jake acknowledged them, confirmed they were important, but then asked to set all that aside right now to focus on their one important goal. Everyone agreed. And suddenly, the antagonistic staff member was neutralized.

Then Jake started going first around the room, inviting people to speak, starting with the shyest person. When someone shy hesitates, try to support them, encourage them, tell them what they have to say is important. Of course, one of the other older workers took the opportunity to interrupt, saying that they had heard all of these ideas before. In response, Jake jumped in to ask to let the shy staffer continue, because in his view she's had some good ideas before. The inconsiderate older guy had nowhere to go after that—he was isolated. So then Jake continued, asking the most junior employees to speak next, then the mid-level staff, and then at last the two older workers who had regularly disrespected their boss and interrupted their colleagues. Interestingly, as it turned out, the older employees were the only two not prepared to speak and offer constructive suggestions—they were so used to only interrupting and disagreeing they hadn't bothered to prepare anything to offer at the meeting:

Now the entire team was looking at them as dead weight. And the older guys were embarrassed in front of everyone.

After that, Jake decided to double down on the meetings, and this team accordingly doubled their productivity. At the end, the younger employees, who would typically be trained privately by the two older staff members, started to suggest to the older guys that they ought to share their wisdom, and the various insights they were sharing privately, with everyone at the meetings. Soon enough, this group started to work together as team. Jake would also reach down to the older guys personally and made it clear that he needed and valued them. The younger employees, for their part, started to feel appreciated at the meetings because they were being heard, and from then on 90 percent of the group was behind Jake as the leader of the team. They would protect him on other projects, and he used these meetings to solidify his team's cooperative spirit.

This is critical: a huge, positive side effect of leading a meeting correctly over time is that you're now starting to build an open culture—no matter what, people know they will be heard. People will be acknowledged in front of everyone else that they did great work. And of course that's what employees want more than anything—to be respected. They know they're heard, appreciated, and ultimately valued, and that encourages them to bring more ideas to the team. All of a sudden, everyone's coming up with great ideas. And in a spirit of openness, hard work, and idea-generation, efficiency rises and increased productivity always follows.

Among the other things accomplished by running efficient meetings is that colleagues see everyone learning to respect other's opinions. Second, once you eliminate the chaos of a poorly run meeting, you can start to see who your high-potential leaders might be emerging from the group. Who's engaging others, who is selling and persuading others about their ideas? What an efficient, great way to accomplish so many goals in an hour each week!

Great team meetings also improve your ability to build trust when you're meeting with individuals one on one. There won't be a dual personality going on—they won't see you as a tough guy in one meeting trying to be a nice guy in a private one. Rather, they'll know who you are, because you consistently act the same way. That's the undisputed hard currency of leadership—consistency in words and actions builds trust.

Leading a meeting correctly isn't just leading a meeting correctly—it's one of the most powerful arenas to accomplish a multitude of goals in a limited time and with a large group of people. It sure beats having to go around after the gathering to meet one on one to find out what everyone actually has to say.

In the preceding story, Jake was a Millennial-age manager, but you don't have to be a young guy to necessarily make big changes.

Daniel, a 49-year-old executive in a mature Fortune 500 major corporation, was a great contributor to his firm and well respected by his superiors. Still, after years, his CTO never felt that he had the "right personality" to lead a team.

Daniel was a thoughtful guy, who looked out for other people and was very good at figuring out whether a new technology was a good fit for his company. Like most brilliant intellectual types, he had a few traits, however, that didn't work well when it came to managing people. His mind moved very fast, and it was very hard for his mouth to keep up with it. He had a tendency to talk quickly and loudly, and he'd logically come to his own conclusions before they made sense to everyone else.

Daniel would leave everyone behind, and people had a tough time following him—he was a classically poor communicator. He'd figure out the answer before everyone else did, and then forcefully and loudly tell everyone that what he thought was the solution and that whatever other argument they'd care to offer naturally wouldn't make any sense. Once Daniel was done, the discussion was over.

Having sat in on some of his meetings, I would have to say that Daniel was right about 98 percent of the time—he was that smart. Knowing this, the CTO would think about promoting him to a management position all the time because of his abilities, but it would always be blocked because of Daniel's "personality"—as if that were something made of stone that could never change.

I was asked to coach Daniel on his communication style. When I first met with him it was pretty clear that he talked a mile a minute and thought everything through on his own before soliciting anyone else's opinions. One of the things I discovered from coaching a lot of bright people, who also were somewhat sensitive by nature, was that in their past they had been shut down or shut out of conversations, their sensitivity contributing to shyness, which made it difficult for them to speak up. Eventually, in order to survive they would overcompensate and become very forceful when communicating, especially if they sensed there was a threat of them not being able to get their ideas or thoughts across. And they had little self-regard for the fact that others perceived their behaviors as obnoxious.

In Daniel's case, his shyness in speaking was severely tested when he entered the military and was forced to speak up as a communications officer in a tank division. He learned quickly that he had to be loud—very loud! And he was in an environment where he had to give orders that people unquestionably had to follow—there's no debate on a military battlefield. This, of course, forced Daniel to overcome his shyness and in fact turned him into a fire breathing speaker. Because loud and unyielding persuasiveness is what helped to build his confidence in war, he naturally continued to speak this way in his postmilitary business meetings—especially if he felt even slightly threatened.

So the first thing we tackled was the emotional trigger that caused him to react so strongly and ignore other's opinions. That deep insecurity of not being heard was holding him back from leading a group. And to lead a group in the corporation was something that he wanted very badly.

At first he argued with me like crazy about how everyone else wasn't making sense in these meetings, or that they were lazy, or they were politically motivated and not thinking about actually solving a problem. It took about three weeks of pointing out that *he* was the one not putting in the effort to listen to others. Instead he was rationalizing his forceful style by positioning them as wrong. I had gained his trust enough that I could be very blunt with him, and he would listen.

Taking a page from his own playbook, I wouldn't let him speak until I was finished, and then I would cut him off as soon as he started defending to me why he had said something in a meeting that ticked someone off. I would point out where he was wrong and tell him he had to accept that he was wrong or there was no point to the coaching. I was blunt, totally black and white about it, and I was very tough on him. He hated this. He sarcastically told me one day that he looked forward to his weekly beating from me. I looked at him when he said this and replied simply that now he knew how it felt to be in a meeting with him.

He reeled for a moment, and then he got it. Again, he was a very smart guy, and once he learned something he didn't forget it. He thought of a word that reminded him of the past and he wrote it on everything—his cell phone, his notepad, and wrote it on a card and stuck it on his bathroom mirror. This made him develop the habit of thinking of that word before he spoke to remind him of the "past" way that he communicated.

At 49, it's hard to change the way you've been doing something for 29 years, so naturally it doesn't change overnight. In Daniel's case it took a couple of months before he had changed the way he normally communicated, and listened to others, including them in his thought process and eliciting their opinions. But he did it, and shortly thereafter he was put in charge of a team of younger and older reports tasked with new product design. Daniel thrived in this position and became a very patient manager. He made sure everyone got a chance to speak in meetings and listened to everyone's ideas before passing judgment on them. His leaders were both shocked, understandably, but also very pleased. They never thought this could possibly happen.

And as good as Daniel was at perceiving corporate politics before we worked together, he became an expert at it afterward. By developing his listening skills, and by gaining the trust of others, he gleaned more information than almost anybody else in his division and was very successful in navigating corporate politics, thereby protecting his team and the projects that he was responsible for. Soon enough, Daniel began giving presentations to the senior management of the company on a regular basis and utilized what he had learned in presenting his group ideas effectively, while answering other executive's questions and embracing their ideas and opinions.

So at 49, Daniel became a successful leader, manager, and communicator, overcoming all of the bad habits and emotional triggers that were holding him back. Clearly, he was able to change the negative aspects of how he worked with others, turning what he was most afraid of (not being heard) and what he did not do well (not listening to and acknowledging others) into his greatest strengths as a manager. And if he can do it, so can you.

Let's return to our key steps in running a meeting. When you're considering your agenda, think hard about what you want to achieve, and what kind of a meeting it is. For example, do you need to resolve issues pertaining to a time-limited project, is it a conceptual brainstorming session, or a review of productivity over past months? In other words, which one of the three broad categories of decision making, idea-generating, or information sharing does your meeting fall under?

From there, work backward to figure out what needs to be discussed to reach your ultimate goal—what questions should be raised and answered, what tasks have to be assigned, and who do you most need to hear from?

With respect to this last point, give careful consideration to those you plan to include in the meeting. How many people need to be there, have they worked together before, and what are their individual agendas? These are especially critical questions—know your audience, find out whether what they need in any way corresponds with your needs. Recall our earlier discussion about matrix management and how to best manage and create value from others over whom you do not have direct authority.

To the extent you can, and to the extent you have some choices, also give consideration to the environment in which you're meeting. The basic idea is to create a space that discourages distractions or interruptions—if it's a long meeting, of course, you'll want to order in some coffee or perhaps lunch, but understand that there are lots of interruptions associated with anything other than the business at hand. You want your participants to be focused on the agenda—don't give them anything else to look at unless necessary, because almost certainly they will be distracted. Seal the room off from outside noise, and at the start of your presentation make a show of not only closing your laptop but silencing your phone too. Let everyone know how serious the meeting you're leading is meant to be.

Have copies of your agenda available, if feasible, and after thanking everyone—which you should always do, every time—remind them of the goals for the particular meeting. Keep everyone on the clock—they'll already be informed that you plan to meet for an hour, for example, but as you move along let everyone know if you're running behind, if they need to pick it up, or generally how much time is left to go. And stick to your agenda—start with the most important item, when everyone's energy is fresh and focused, and resist the temptation to take care of "the easy things" first.

The conclusion of your meeting is also a critical time to redirect focus. Wrap it up by restating what you think the team just accomplished, list all the to-do items that were agreed upon, acknowledge the matters that were brought up that you determined to be outside of the focus of the respective meeting, and reassure the group members that these will be revisited, and assign responsibilities. And, as you opened the meeting with appreciation for their attendance, close it with a similar expression of sincere gratitude.

What happens when events demand that you have to call a quick meeting, often in crisis or under some other emergency, or suddenly time-constrained situation? Well, all that careful planning I'm suggesting here won't be possible to do, but at the same time you don't want to become inconsistent in tone with your staff.

My advice to people in this position goes back to a journalism course I took as an undergraduate student long ago: when writing a lead to a news story, consider the who, what, when, where, and why of it. Who should be at the meeting, what's it going to be about, when will it be held, where will it be held, and why is it important? Communicate that in your e-mail to your staff, and encourage them to be ready to speak if called upon. What do you need answered from them? If you know before the meeting, then let them know that too.

Deploying strategic compassion, controlling your triggers, and leading your staff with genuine concern builds a culture of open communications that Millennials expect and that, frankly, leads in the 21st century to total business success.

Chapter 10

Creating the Culture You Want

And Breaking Down the One You Don't Want

The culture of a company is to its employees what a brand might be to potential customers. It's what motivates your workers to make your vision for the business their own, and it's what compels them to devote so much of their day to their responsibilities and, ultimately, to the productivity and profitability of your firm.

Almost every successful company is concerned about its culture. Indeed, the culture at a particular company often is impressed upon the entire corporation, even for generations, by its founders, innovators, and pioneer leaders. At times, of course, a corporate culture sort of natural blossoms on its own. But like an untended garden, a spontaneously blooming culture isn't often a healthy or open one. It needs to be tended to, pruned, and nurtured if it is to stay on course. And that responsibility, like all others discussed in this work, will be on the shoulders of the leaders with vision and inner strength.

We can look at culture as the sum expression of all the interactions the employees of a firm are having with one another. Are you contributing in a meaningful way to the presentation of the company's preferred attitudes? And are those attitudes and resultant behaviors in support of your company's basic mission? Is your corporate culture open? Is it dynamic? Does it reflect the central values and how you hold yourself out both to present and potential employees, and to your investors and customers?

If you're in the enviable position of founding your own firm, and thus facing a clean slate to establish your own imprint on your company's culture, then you'll need to consider (1) what that culture should be and (2) how will you enfranchise your employees to interact in ways that are consistent with that vision, or—even better—encourage them to "buy in" to such an extent that they make your culture vision their own.

But let's say you're not a company founder. Let's say you're a new manager, or a Millennial executive, and you're in a work environment that already has a deeply rooted culture. And let's say you don't particularly care for that culture. Can you change it? It's not easy, but yes—and you do it by localizing your own open vision within the team of the employees that you manage by following these points, all of which are critical components:

1. Create an open culture that's transparent and fosters communications in all directions.
2. Be consistent and take responsibility for your actions.
3. If possible, try to hire people who would appear to share the values of your firm or department.
4. Provide opportunities for mentoring.

Very few successful companies in the 21st century are able to make it without having established an open corporate culture. Google, famously, has set the standard for its ability to maintain a sort of start-up cultural ethic throughout its offices worldwide. The whole idea at Google is to create environments that foster the sharing of ideas and opinions. This makes perfect sense for a cutting-edge tech companies employing thousands of brilliant people—a creative, open environment promoting communications and idea development is critical to its success. Google office spaces tend to be artful, whimsical, and comfortable, and there are many opportunities for small groups of people to meet, converse, and exchange opinions. It is no exaggeration that Google's culture is the lifeblood of the company's development and contributes directly to its profitability.

So if you're looking to create an open culture, whether in your start up or within your group, the first thing to do is to be clear about your vision. Write it down. Be explicit, and keep the language simple—don't use acronyms, for example, that are known to only a few people. Such practices help to create silos, and the idea of a successful culture is one for which communications are easy and encouraged. In your vision statement, express clearly what attitudes are valued by your company—and maybe even which ones aren't.

As in all matters, it's the leader's behavior and actions that will have the most impact on the establishment of a corporate culture. Do as you say—be consistent, and set the tone for your company or group by your repeated and unvaried behavior. Whether it's leading a meeting or setting a career path for a junior worker, control your emotional triggers at all times and practice what you preach. And if someone starts to express a negative attitude that contrasts with the agreed-upon culture, you need to speak with that individual and nip that in the bud before ethos in your company becomes infected. Negativity in a company can spread like a cancer.

Trust, of course, within all the interpersonal relationships in your group is critical to the establishment of an open culture. And how you start is typically how you're going to end, so ideally you want to establish a good culture right from the beginning. Undoing a culture that's been there for a while isn't impossible, but it's very difficult.

You'll know right away when a corporate culture is a bad one—you'll experience mistrust, backstabbing, silos, and political, Machiavellian behavior. Think back to the Buddhist hierarchy of life conditions known as the Ten Worlds—people without a shared vision thrown together into a workplace will naturally default to function as self-centered, animalistic individuals. They're out for themselves, and they will undermine others if it creates an advantage for them. Work becomes a long-running episode of "Survivor." A bad culture also is usually obvious in a meeting where people start blaming other groups right away for not getting something done. They're literally splitting up the company on their own, a war inside the company. They're competing but based only on protecting themselves—not on creating value for the company.

In such an environment people hold back information. How can you successfully run a company if you don't have voluminous and clear information? You will then have to dig to find out the truth. How much time in the day do you have to do this? But if you put the time in now to create an open culture, it'll pay off later. You have to set a standard for this culture, you have to tell everyone that holding back information isn't useful—and will be punished. Not hearing everybody, not giving people an opportunity to speak, not acknowledging people will create tension among your staff. You also have to communicate—tell people what you're facing and come up with a plan to fix it. Otherwise if you just drop an ax on people, the rest of the company will wonder what's going on due to your betrayal of trust.

A good culture is an open culture—but thoughtfully open. This doesn't mean one in which you can say whatever you want to other people. A good culture aligns company goals with the personal goals of its employees. It's one where people know that they're respected and acknowledged. It's also where people take responsibility themselves to know what they should be doing, rather than being told what to do.

It's human nature for people to hold on, to get paranoid, to make things up in their heads—it's baked into people in general but also into corporate culture specifically. The important thing is that you're prepared to handle challenges to your culture as soon as they come up. If you fail to deal with an overt problem right away, people start to assume that such behavior is acceptable. And people will take advantage of that. You have to have the courage as a leader to actually talk to people about any critical transgression and stop it right there. But do this in a way that's based on all the strategically compassionate tools we've already covered.

First, let them know they have an agenda that won't work here. Second, show them how it's in the best interest not to have that agenda. Tell them, essentially, "how you go about your business is fine, but here's how we do it here." If the issue is that someone's gunning for someone else's job, and if they're a worthy employee otherwise, then help them to develop a better plan. By acknowledging the person struggling with your corporate culture, you diffuse their agenda: they know now that they'll be going against the boss; their actions, they now understand, are not in their best interest; and, finally, you're offering them a way to crawl back from way out on that limb. In any event, don't corner them. If you just criticize someone without giving him or her a path back, you may be right but you're dead right—you'll be dead, you've not given the individual a path back.

Still, when a manager is being phony, dishonest, political, and they're in a position of authority, people fear them—you as the leader of that company has to call them out—and if they leave, so be it.

A good corporate culture is one in which people don't hammer each other. If someone is overly critical, well of course they may be right. Perhaps someone is screwing up, maybe they have to change their behavior, or work harder, or better develop their skills, and so on—that's all work stuff. The important thing is how you communicate all of this.

By not paying attention to the people working for you and not showing them how you want them to behave they will create a corporate culture on their own—and it won't likely be the one you'd prefer. Would you like to see people cornered or hammered in public? That's a culture too. It's called the United States Marine Corps.

If you allow this to happen at your workplace, a negative culture will take off on its own. Then you'll have to correct it. You can, however, create local cultures within a larger corporate culture. It's very good to start with a small group, then when it does well there's an example that people will take note of—productivity goes up, they get raises and promotions, and senior management rewards them.

It's basically the pebble in the pond theory. If you try to take on a company as a whole you'll either create more infighting or end up getting fired. Rather, if things are heading in a bad direction, find a few folks and create a local example to accomplish something good.

Where would you like to work, and how would you like to feel? Put yourself in the shoes of the people working there, what would they want? Everyone has different backgrounds skills and motivations. If you already know what they do, and you know the industry, and you know what your workers consider to be their optimal work environment, then start right there. Institutionalize a culture that's already productive and make it so they want to continue to be there. Whatever the culture, people will either adapt or they're going to be gone, along with whatever talent they might have had.

It's hard to change an entrenched, negative culture. People resist change, even if they understand the change to be beneficial. They become fearful and anxious and wonder if they're going to lose power and influence. Maybe they think they'd rather stay with the dysfunction they know well than invite in the possibility of new, unknown problems. This is all a part of human nature, so expect it.

Figure out where the existing problems lie—are they personnel, policies, or communication issues? Try to convince people who are hesitant what the long-term effects of inaction might be—and how will such inaction ultimately affect both the bottom line and their own job security. And, of course, provide where possible incentives for everyone to change.

Find people in your environment to move up the ladder. You can't do it with everyone because sometimes you will need certain skills. But as you grow and develop, people can learn the business and step up. People want to know if they have an opportunity to learn stuff and move up without being suppressed or depressed. Millennials are especially looking for this. And this is why mentoring in business is becoming more and more critical to success.

A mentor helps you to perceive your own weaknesses and confront them with courage. The bond between the mentor and the student, depending upon the strength of the relationship and the connection, enables the less experienced worker to stay true his or her chosen career path until he or she reaches his or her goals.

Mentoring is an ancient concept, and there's a reason it's still employed—it functions splendidly as an organizational practice in which people work together to learn, develop, and transfer specific skill sets. Quite apart from contemporary corporate culture, mentoring is a strong component of religion, sports, apprentice trades, and many other of life's most important endeavors. In Buddhism, just as an example, the mentoring relationship dates back at least 3,000 years during which the Buddha's teachings were orally communicated for some 600 years before they were even written down.

Some people are anxious about having a mentor, not wanting any other person of authority perhaps to get quite too close. But mentor and student is not master and slave—in a master-slave relationship, the slave exists to support the master and must do his or her bidding under threat of punishment. In a mentor-student relationship, the mentor supports the student. At most, he or she might speak to the student in a direct manner in an effort to correct him or her.

In the workplace, mentoring is the method by which new leaders are discovered and trained. It's hard to find a great business mentor, so when you do hold on to them. Such a person should be very skilled in your field, kind, sensitive to what you're potentially capable of achieving, able to make tough choices, and courageous enough to have your back if something goes wrong.

The preceding description, of course, is how we've also come to understand leadership in the context of strategic compassion. And while I don't at all mean to underestimate the importance of business knowledge and competency, leadership in the workplace is even more about emotional maturity and character.

As we progress deeper into the 21st century, the need for education will continue to grow. The economy will only become more knowledge-based. Workers will need to constantly be educated, and not necessarily through traditional methods of schooling. Rather, companies will have to build into their cultures a learning subculture to put themselves ahead of the curve and be ready for what's next. This means more mentoring, both so that workers know the company is investing in them but also so the younger workers become strong and capable resources for the future.

Mentoring in and of itself improves your open culture, because mentoring is inherently predicated on human connections. You can't really mentor by phone or e-mail. You need to be together in the enterprise, eye to eye, putting individuals on the firmest ground to develop their personal capacities in the most humanistic context.

Mentoring is perhaps the smartest way to do business, because it allows your company to continue to grow, to raise leaders, and to be prepared to adapt to future challenges. Mentoring has been often reported to lead to "increased rates of employee retention, improved morale, increased organizational commitment and job satisfaction, accelerated leadership development, better succession planning, reduced stress, stronger and more cohesive teams, and heightened individual and organizational learning."[1]

An excellent mentor will appear in your life from time to time, and then either you or the mentor will move on—or be replaced, if you're fortunate, by someone else. The wisdom and training he or she imparts, however, should plant seeds that will germinate for a lifetime. In my view, mentoring is a critical component of a successful and open corporate culture.

A marketing firm I worked with had only been in business for three years when it started to grow at a fantastic rate. This company was founded by a CEO who came from a large corporation, and initially the company had a small number of loyal employees who had some experience but not a great deal of training. As the company started to get more work, everyone was given the opportunity to take on new roles and responsibilities.

Basically, the CEO himself would have to train everyone. There were a few employees who had more experience, and from time to time they would help in the training as well. The CEO naturally started running out of time to train anybody as the business grew in leaps and bounds. Accordingly, more senior managers were hired from larger companies.

Right away the CEO included in their job descriptions that they would have to help train the less experienced workers and that the policy of the company was to promote from within if at all possible. Some of these new hires balked a little at having to do this. They felt they already had a tough job with plenty to do, and would ask why they couldn't just hire experienced people instead of training the existing employees.

The CEO took the time to explain his philosophy of investing in people and then getting the return on investment over time. He would tell them that having the trust and loyalty of the staff many times outweighed experience. About two-thirds of the senior hires stayed with the company; the rest were either let go or quit. They were just too indoctrinated with a survival of the fittest attitude and couldn't get behind training the less experienced staff—all of whom were of Millennial age.

About six months later, the company exploded with even more new clients. Finally, a hiring manager was brought on board, and they started recruiting at a rapid rate. Here is what's so interesting: all of the employees, instead of feeling threatened, helped to develop a plan for training the new hires, even the ones who were above them! They were all more concerned with the company being successful and profitable than worrying about themselves. Don't get me wrong—they were Millennials, so after many of the new people had settled in you better believe they asked the CEO what their new path would be at the company if it wasn't already defined for them. Most of them, however, as you might suspect, already had had a path set forth for them by this savvy CEO.

To this day, the culture at the company is one of unity and open communications. When problems crop up, everyone openly discusses them and comes up with a solution. The company is still growing at lightning speed, and although everyone has basically got more to do than is possible they are incredibly successful. And in a terrific indication that they're on the right path, right now 80 percent of their new business derives from referral rather than direct marketing.

Succession planning is also an important component of a healthy corporate culture and long-term planning. An obstacle arises with succession planning, of course, to the extent that the person charged with preparing a successor is doing so in advance of his or her own replacement. I don't even like to use the term succession planning, but in any event make sure you figure out first what's next for the more senior individual before you ask him or her to train someone for their respective job. If you don't, don't expect your succession plan to work.

A good culture is one that sustains for many years. And a healthy, happy culture does wonders for a corporate brand. Companies like Virgin or Qualcomm—where employees are provided with exercise spaces and are encouraged to come and go as they please as long as the work gets done—want their employees to be happy and healthy. Google, as mentioned, is an open culture because they need ideas every day. When you build from the ground up based on how workers become successful and happy, then you build a legacy that goes on. People will not challenge the culture or think the mission statement is lip service if that's how it really works there. Whatever culture you build, if it's based on helping people grow, which keeps your company growing, then you've developed the right culture and people want to work there.

As with other major work innovations, you've got to be courageous and strong. Decide what you're going to build and then stay the course regardless of pressure from investors, outsiders or your managers. And you'll get it from anyone with his or her own agenda who doesn't care about the whole organization like you do. Apply all the math and finance to back up why the culture you're implementing makes the best business sense. A humanistic culture that really puts its people first saves a ton of money in having clear and honest communication alone. And it enhances efficiency by diminishing the silos and turf wars that result from departments and individuals within the company competing in a negative way with each other.

There are most certainly people, perhaps in most companies, who would allow their colleagues to fail if they think it will make them look better. But failures cost the company money. Managers holding back information and not helping other departments cost the company money. Staff not supporting their managers cost the company money. People not liking the culture where they work cost a fortune! Their performance is lower and they are not going to be loyal to senior management or the company. They will leave at the first opportunity. Replacing people costs the company more money!

I'm reiterating all of this so you can build the case you need to with everyone at your company in order to establish and build the culture you want.

As you start this journey people (especially more experienced ones) may tend to revert to a "me first" attitude because this may be what they were taught in the work environment they started their career as a method to survive. That's exactly when you have to step in right away! Don't wait and let them think it's even remotely possible that a selfish, politically motivated attitude will be tolerated.

When I was a small boy, my neighbor, Bob Prescott, was the man who founded the Flying Tigers air cargo line, which later was folded into Federal Express. His son was my best friend. He was what you would call a "natural leader"—one of the original "flying tigers" in World War II and an ace, having shot down more than five enemy planes in battle. In one particular skirmish, his fighter group was greatly outnumbered by the Japanese fighter planes, who were slaughtering the Chinese on the ground.

Mr. Prescott's fighter group came up with a unique formation that actually made them stick together when they attacked the Japanese fighter planes. The American P40s were not as maneuverable as the Japanese Zeroes, so this was the only way they could beat them.

As a result, the much smaller group of U.S. fighter planes attacked in formation, sticking together, and managed to down enough Japanese fighters to stop the attacks on the Chinese. That kind of teamwork, trust, and loyalty was exactly the culture Mr. Prescott instituted when he founded his company. When politics and badmouthing would flare up between managers at the airline (as would happen anywhere), he'd call both of the managers into his office and order the one who came to him first to tell the other what he'd just told the boss. That of course quickly put a stop to any badmouthing and undermining.

The message was crystal clear: if you open your mouth it had better be true, and you'd better be able to back it up. Now and then, I'm sure, there would be a battle in the office, but in the end he never let anyone leave without resolving it. That airline suffered a number of financial crises, and several unexplained crashes that would have made other airlines go out of business. Most people credit the survival and eventual success of the Flying Tiger line to Bob Prescott's honest and forthright leadership skills. The culture endured until he passed away after running the airline for several decades. He was the first and the last president, right up until the time it merged with Federal Express.

What's the ultimate lesson here? Never, ever let go of the good culture you build. Stick with it through thick and thin. You'll inspire the same behavior in the people you lead, and then they will pass it on to the next group of managers.

And while free food, and I suppose bowling lanes, are generous benefits, that's not what really promises a sustainable and open corporate culture. Corporate culture is not really that kind of a luxury—it's a luxury because it's often neglected, but what actually makes for a terrific culture where people truly want to work is open communications and the opportunities to be mentored. Create a culture that stimulates innovation, rewards the development of inner strength, promotes collaboration, attracts customers and increases profitability, and builds a winning mentality.

Your commitment to your corporate vision will ultimately make your business work and attract and retain the best people to your firm.

It has to be constantly tended to, and so take the pulse of your company as much as possible. For sure, your weekly meeting, if you lead one, will be a great opportunity to gauge exactly what's going on, but also meet with individuals on a regular basis and informally talk with them.

The opportunities for informal talk, which are critical means for obtaining important and honest information, are often promoted by installing informal eating areas, such as a large and well-stocked kitchen, where people might sit, relax, and talk. These areas are also useful because they are void of symbols of authority—you don't have to be the boss, but more like a friend or colleague, when you're sitting down on the couch in a common area for a cup of tea.

So be diligent when you hire new people, or when you've instituted a new culture in your already-existing departments. Make sure your people are clear about your vision for how the company expects to be run. Keep your door open for communications. Invest in your younger employees, always let them know they're appreciated, and provide for them real mentoring opportunities.

Moreover, believe in your heart that Millennial workers want these opportunities. I remember once chatting with a doctor during a personal medical visit. He had asked me what I do, and he seemed intrigued by the idea that I coach people with a particular interest in the Millennial corporate culture. He looked around and said, "Yeah, we've got a lot of Millennials here. You see some who have potential and some who don't." I thought to myself, man, you're really missing the point. Someone maybe is naturally leading someone around, but others might have that potential too. Making instantaneous judgments from the outside is not leadership. Getting in there and nurturing people is.

NOTE

1. Lois J. Zachary, *Creating a Mentoring Culture: The Organization's Guide* (Hoboken, NJ: Jossey-Bass, 2005).

Chapter 11

Becoming the Complete Leader

The Art of Communication

Throughout this work we've examined the following components of what makes a complete and successful businessperson in the Millennial age: the importance of emotional intelligence, the control of emotional triggers, the view of people as your most important resource, the concepts of strategic compassion, the differences between leading and managing, the best defenses to war in today's contemporary business environment, the art of leading a meeting, and the critical importance of creating and maintaining an open corporate culture. All of this, of course, is in the service of becoming a terrific business leader—one who is efficient, productive, and successful.

What lies at the bottom of all these techniques and strategies? What's the one thing they pretty much all have in common? That would have to be the ability to deal with people—how to read them; how to forge valuable relationships with them; how to most effectively communicate; and how to nurture a shared, long-term vision for growth and development.

Learning how to communicate well is a terrific skill that some leaders have and others don't. But it's one of those things that you can always work on, if you put in the effort to gradually improve. It'll take some time, especially if you tend to be shy, but if you challenge yourself at least a bit every day, you'll see conspicuous results over a period of weeks or months.

Fortunately, the primary root to great communications has nothing to do with how well you speak—that's the easier part, and you can always develop that later. Rather, the quickest way to improve your communication talents is to first nurture a sincere capacity to care about what the other person is saying. In other words, the main key to relating to other people is to listen to what they have to say.

Sounds easy, doesn't it? It's not. Listening isn't hearing; listening includes hearing the words that are being spoken, but it's also about picking up the nonverbal communication associated with them. What's the other person's body language telling you? With what tone are they presenting their words? Are they angry, frustrated, sad, or happy? Are they bragging, or possibly covering up their insecurities by projecting overconfidence? Don't prepare to necessarily respond to others, especially if they're sharing with you important, detailed information about their business performance. Concentrate instead on listening to what they have to say. And reflect in your mind on all the things they're saying, together with the nuances of how they physically appear—their mood, the tone of their voice, and all of the innumerable ways we communicate with each other in all of our complexities. If they say something that you don't understand, then ask for a clarification so that there's no confusion.

An important aspect of good business communications is the ability to empathize with others. Empathy, in one sense, is the ability to show respect to another, and a lot of what we've discussed in this work is precisely grounded on developing respect for those with whom you work. Can you reassure another individual that you hear what he or she is saying? Can you put yourself in their shoes and understand what's causing them distress, what they think needs to be improved, or what at times you might need to do to make their situation more productive and efficient?

At a SWOT meeting, or during any one-on-one dialogue, whether formal or informal, people may very well tell you things that you don't want to hear. A lot of people are shocked when this happens, and they feign not ever being aware of the respective issue or problem. Still even more people will succumb to their emotional triggers. "What did you say about me?" is, at least in most places, the prelude to a larger fight. But don't go there. As mentioned, strategic compassion is a difficult process, and if you're going to really reach in and communicate with your reports—which is what they, as Millennials, want you to do—then you have to be prepared to hear all of what they have to say.

Control your emotions and reflect on what you've learned. You don't need to answer anyone right away, depending of course on the context of the conversation, but make sure you let the other people know that you're listening and you hear them—whether the news was good or not.

In general you'll want to try to make everyone feel welcomed, appreciated, and respected. Don't be cheap with your praise—praise doesn't make anyone lazy, it makes them only want to work harder. That's why I always try to thank everyone—the administrative staff, the security guys, the food service people—everyone. If you surround yourself in a cloud of gratitude, then that spirit of appreciation will come right back to you. And you also never know whom you're speaking to and where they might someday end up.

I recall some work I did years ago for an investment group trying to develop a mountainous piece of property so that certain educational objectives they were supporting could expand. A lot of local activists were against what they wanted to do—the development plan itself was environmentally sensitive, but they were in an area in which building generally was restricted. It was a tough fight for both sides, and a lot of money was spent, perhaps unnecessarily, on lawyers, lobbyists, and PR consultants. They probably could have worked the whole thing out by pursuing a more savvy and open channel of communications, but neither side was ever quite comfortable enough with the other and so for year after year they remained at each other's throats, and nothing was able to change.

The point of this story is not so simple as the parties finally figuring out how to communicate. They never really did, and the final disposition of the fight ended up as a political decision. What's of interest, though, is that the property owners had for years retained a rather humble community relations consultant, whose job it was to cultivate good relationships with local elected officials. For years this guy would visit government offices, and after a while he became friendly not so much with the politicians themselves necessarily, but with their staffs—the receptionists, the secretaries, the drivers, and others. And during each visit the consultant would show up just to say hello bearing small presents for the staff—flowers, chocolates, that sort of thing. Well, when the consultant's clients needed to meet directly with the elected officials, who do you think smoothed the way for this to happen? The receptionists, the secretaries, and the drivers did. The appropriate support staff made sure to put the consultant on the politician's schedule. And in the case of the property owners I knew, it was precisely through these relationships that a certain elected official came to understand the issues that were at stake, and it was he who helped to finally resolve the land use matter. So just because someone doesn't have an authoritative or conspicuous position, don't ever take that person for granted.

Once you've perfected the ability to listen, you can't just sit there of course and stare at the person across from you. You need to consider what to say and how to say it. Don't overthink things, of course—just communicate clearly and say what needs to be said. Be direct, be honest, and always be respectful. Be aware of differences in culture, and be cognizant about what you already know about the person with whom you're speaking—what are his or her triggers? Look them in the eyes, use open, non-defensive body language, and basically trust in who you are as a leader. You don't need to be anyone else but yourself.

As we know by now, being a leader takes courage. You're going to have to correct people, train them sometimes, and unfortunately also sometimes let them go. What you want to make sure of is that you've done your best to resolve problems and issues with them.

Smart managers resolve issues as quickly as possible to get back on track and stay productive. Ignoring and not dealing with someone who has a problem or an issue only builds resentment, which in turn degrades performance. On the other hand, dealing with an issue sends a clear message that you're paying attention and you're concerned.

A department at one of the tech companies where I was coaching was headed by a brilliant software engineer named Jennifer. Unfortunately, the department had both morale and performance issues. Jennifer would constantly bring up to her staff the many problems she was seeing. Patiently, she'd address what needed to be corrected, how to correct it, and when it needed to be done by. If one engineer couldn't cut it, she'd switch that one out and assign a different engineer to the project. The whole department became a bad version of musical chairs, which of course diminished morale throughout the group. No one was happy with this scenario, and the conditions were progressively worsening.

The first thing Jennifer told me was how uncomfortable she was when it came to engaging people one on one. And she admitted that that's why she had been moving people around instead of talking to them directly about the nature of their issue or performance problem. I asked her if there was a boss in her past who had helped her to overcome a similar problem. She thought of someone right away. I then asked in what ways this boss had assisted her, and she said that he'd oversee what she was doing and when he spotted the problem he would take her to lunch and discuss how to resolve it. Ultimately, he'd figure out what the issue really was—lack of knowledge, experience, or both. Jennifer said she felt completely comfortable telling him what her challenges were, because he would always help her to find a solution. We then talked about the people reporting to her.

I asked what the problems were with each one of them. She told me what they had done wrong, and that she would switch people midstream because, in her opinion, the new person had a better possibility of getting it right. Then I asked if she actually knew what each of them were capable of doing, since she was aware only of the one skill that they were initially hired for. We then came up with a plan for Jennifer to take each one of them to lunch and, discuss what they liked doing and what they weren't sure of. Then she'd bring up the particular problem they needed to solve and either teach them how to solve it or get them to someone who could train them.

As she instituted the plan, she discovered, indeed, that some of them had skills she didn't know about that could help her group. She also realized that some of the development requests her department was getting were not clear enough and would force her team to guess instead of ask her what they meant—because they were too afraid to ask her. She also perceived in some cases what skills people still needed to develop, and she did her best to come up with a plan to help them learn these. Most importantly, she got to know them as people, not just software engineers.

The results were as expected—performance improved. Jennifer instituted a policy to spend at least 15 minutes with any engineer who was struggling with a challenge before determining the best course of action. She told me that 75 percent of the time the issues were resolved by the engineer without putting anyone else on it. And now her staff was proactively coming to her with problems before they turned into major issues.

Whether you identify as a manager or a leader, you have to be proactive. You can't let small problems fester, or they will grow into larger ones. In this regard, you've got to take actions immediately if you perceive that something is amiss.

This awareness of when to take swift action is another subtle aspect of excellent leadership. This doesn't mean that you should be unthinking—I've seen executives become whirlwinds of action, but without thought those actions don't add up to much. You of course have to think before you act. But when you've identified a problem—for example, a person or persons behaving outside of the cultural norm you've established—don't wait. No one else is coming to help.

In one sense, thinking with strategic compassion is essentially the difference between dealing with what's in front of your face versus what's coming in the future. Again, a manager tends to be reactive; a leader, on the other hand, is proactive. But to be proactive, you need to develop the necessary strategies for the future with the people that you have right now. If you don't have an end goal in sight, it's so easy to get lost along the way; you're vulnerable to distractions, and you will lose your perspective—that's human nature. Instead, develop a good strategy for where you want your team to be in 6 months, 12 months, 18 months, two years, and beyond.

Please don't be like the executives who would hire George Clooney in the film *Up In the Air*! In that movie, Clooney is a guy retained by corporations to break the news to employees that they've been fired. Talk to your reports. Make sure they know where you're coming from, and what your expectations are. And if they need to be let go, don't allow it to come out of the blue—make sure that you've made every effort to put them on track so that they could be productive. After all, there is enormous waste in firing someone and spending all the financial and work-hour resources to find someone else.

Another important angle associated with all of these communications and management techniques is to make sure you follow up with the people you're working with them on.

Nobody's going to perfectly grasp a technique or skill the first time around. Just like anything, it takes practice. What is crucial, though, is that you make the time to follow up with them a short time later and that you do it consistently until they know they've mastered it.

After all, trust is built on being consistent, dependable, and credible. When you say you'll follow up with them, make sure you do it or the end result could be worse than before you started the respective work.

One of the managers I coached at a tech company had a team of client service employees whose performances were deteriorating rapidly. The company had launched a new service that was more complicated than the one they had formerly been helping customers with. The CS team was graded on how many customers they helped daily. Lori was the CS manager; she was the one to make sure that the client call-ins were handled, and that the numbers never dropped. The problem was that about a third of the team didn't have a complete grasp about how the new service worked. So although the call volume increased, so did customer complaints because they had to call twice sometimes to get the help they needed.

When I first started working with Lori her problem solving technique was to answer the team member's questions and then move on. She unrealistically thought they would get it right away. She'd become impatient with team members when they asked for more clarity or information. As a result of her style, people stopped asking when they needed help because they were intimidated by her. In fact, a couple of them just up and quit. So Lori had two issues: an emotional response triggered by impatience; and a failure to adequately problem-solve with team members.

We worked on this and devised a system where Lori would spend one-on-one time with team members before and after shifts, sometimes working with two or three people at a time because they had the same questions. Lori also got control of her impatience and was very happy when she realized it was taking her *less* time overall to improve team performance when she spent *more* time working with individual team members on training.

Everything got better. Team members knew that they were responsible for learning how the new services worked, but they also now knew they had Lori supporting them to help them learn. Call volume remained robust, and customer complaints dropped significantly.

I checked in with Lori about six months later, after we had finished, just to see how everything was going. I was shocked when she told me that matters had gone downhill. The company had launched three new services since I last saw her, and the amount of customer complaints had risen again. Everyone in her group was under tremendous pressure. The company had hired 10 new CS representatives to keep up with increased demand.

So naturally I asked her if she was still meeting with team members before and after shifts. She said yes, but only with the new team members, because the existing members she had already spent time with *seemed* to her to be doing just fine and learning on their own. I asked her to look up which reps were getting the most complaints. It turned out that 6 out of 10 were part of the existing team member group. They weren't getting it, and they were not getting the time with Lori anymore.

Lori had stopped following up with them on a consistent basis, and their performance dropped. And, of course, once she got back in to start working with them again, the complaints dropped. It took her more time, and she was already very busy, but eventually things got better.

The point of the story is that you have to keep following up with people until you're sure, and they're sure, they understand and know what to do.

Head off problems before they occur. Instead of waiting to find out that someone doesn't know how to do something, it's far better to proactively tee up a procedure about how to go about the task—offer them an opportunity to get the coaching to do it well right away. This especially holds true when you hire from the outside: you want to immediately sit with your new hires and go through with them how we work here, how our team functions—and ask them if they have other ideas. They need to know exactly how you work. If they come in with their own ideas and then attempt to apply them without any discussion, everyone will think it's incredibly disrespectful—no one will support that.

The most valuable thing on Earth is time, not money. The people working for you are investing their time as well, so include them in the process to keep performance high, morale high, and turnover low.

Don't ever avoid engaging. Utilize what you've learned in your various SWOT analyses to determine what your staff needs to develop to get them to where you expect them to be.

Critically, you have got to set standards—one thing I find when I start coaching is that everyone knows what they're pretty much supposed to do, but often there are no standards set. In engineering there are, of course, and there are clear product guidelines, but I don't see it as much in the realm of office procedures.

This is a leader's job. Obviously you want to set a high standard, though not an unrealistic one. However technically you do it is up to you, but when people first come to a company and you know what you're trying to accomplish, you should be able to say here's the standard we're looking for, here's how we do things. This is acceptable; this is not.

Setting a standard is like setting a goal; it's like seeing a flag on the green. Many times people complain about performance, but it's much easier to first come up with where they need to be, and then they can figure out how to get there. This also eliminates conflict or confusion caused by the standard not being clear.

With Millennials in general, I see people shift gears all the time, they change priorities at the drop of a hat. What happens at this point is that some people panic. You can't just turn a team on a dime; you have to consider where they are on a project. Emergencies are emergencies, of course, but obstacles don't necessarily demand dramatic personnel transformations.

More often than not, I'll observe a young employee working on the project that gets perhaps halfway through a project before dashing into the boss's office to ask what he or she should do next. But that's more like babysitting than mentoring—this irritates a boss and saps his or her energy and time. Much like the case when parents do too much of their kid's own schoolwork, this sort of relationship prevents the less experienced people in a firm from working on developing skills needed to figure out themselves how to accomplish their tasks. That boss isn't getting paid to work with them—they're working for him.

Since CEOs complain about this all the time, how, as an employee, are you supposed to take advantage of a boss's wisdom? Take the project all the way to completion, or as close as you can get it—do your own research, talk to your peers first, and get as close as you possibly can. Then walk into the boss's office with the project. Instead of the supervisor having to get under the hood with you, he or she can then give you the overview and benefit of his experience. It's much quicker and much more efficient. Under this scenario you're taking advantage of both aspects implicit in the mentoring relationship—you're utilizing the boss' knowledge while also driving forward on your own.

People sense whether you know where you're going or not. That breeds feelings of being looked out for, or not. When you engage with your employees, when you find out their aspirations and set them on a career path that's consistent with your company's vision, you're aligning personal growth goals to the company and your team. With a career growth path in mind for each individual, you can plan a critical path based on where they need to be in order for you to expand the team or take on more work. Now you've got an overall strategic plan for your team and each team member.

Moreover, you've got a distinct way forward—you can refer to it and see where your reports need to be along the way. This is a far more effective way to monitor progress as compared to waiting for an annual review.

Helping to plot a detailed career path for your team itself makes you a compelling leader, always moving forward, always looking down the road to where you're supposed to go. Like Bill Clinton once famously said, people elect presidents to look around the corner to see what's coming. The more you can align your team goals with personal goals the more successful you're going to be. This isn't always easy, but in most cases there will be overlaps, there will be ways to match up a person's desires for his or her career with the larger corporate objective. Then you can grow together.

This is what constitutes a happy culture.

Additionally, it's far less expensive to grow your own people than to go outside: the benefits are multiplied because you've already established trust and consistency, and you know what they can do. All of this allows you to enhance the performance of your division or company and make it more sustainable. Swapping people out is very disruptive and expensive.

Give your team a sense of mission. Define what the mission of the team is, and if you instill that sense in them they're going to be self-motivated and efficient. The primary motivation for all of this is so you can continue to inspire people to perform.

With respect to the concept of nurturing your own staff, remember that people are going to follow not just your mouth but your back. Where are *you* going? When you really focus and put the time in to communicate with and raise people underneath you, to make sure that they develop a humanistic leadership style that's part of the culture of your team, and you make the effort to help them get there—as things progress, and the company gets bigger, those people you raised are going to come to you in turn to understand how to train the new people joining in. Now you've created a self-sustaining leadership model that's based on what you wanted in the first place, without having to reinvent the wheel every time new staff is hired. This is the ideal: an open environment that's established, institutionalized, and followed to help the new recruits seamlessly fit into your culture.

Open communications in your corporate culture is the lifeblood of your business. It allows for a free flow of ideas, which in turn increases productivity, efficiency, and performance.

Chapter 12

Why Compassionate Leadership Is in Your Self-Interest

The goal of establishing and running a business is to make money. All the techniques we've reviewed in this work are in the service of this objective. That's not to say that people go into business for other reasons; of course they do. They want to build something lasting and of value, they want to have fun doing it, and they want to contribute some good to the economy and to society in general. But let's face it—most of us in business have a dream to become rich. And all of us who own shares in public companies had better hope that's what the directors of those corporations want for us too.

In order to succeed in business you need to be smart, you'll sometimes want to take risks, and you need to understand the environment and the times in which you find yourself. A radical generational shift has taken place in the past 10–15 years, and it's bound to continue for at least the next 10 years. That is, the Millennials have come to dominate the workforce in this country, and they've brought with them new sensitivities and ways of doing business. Like all good businesspeople, it's up to the rest of us to adapt to how things change—not how we want them to be, and especially not how we fondly remember them to be.

If it takes a more genuine understanding of compassion toward each other, then at least this aspect of the generational revolution is welcomed. The fact is, when we support others, we ourselves are actually being supported; when we help others, we ourselves are actually being helped. This view is rooted in the Buddhist concept of dependent origination, but when applied to business—a seemingly un-Buddhist-like world—it can be expressed as strategic compassion.

Showing others consideration leads to increased profits, because people are motivated to work hard when they feel appreciated, respected, and fulfilled. They will function more efficiently if they're not busy complaining, backbiting, or spending half the day looking for a new job. You'll save money by getting the most out of your people, and you'll save time by not having to constantly interview and hire replacements. Low turnover contributes significantly to the bottom line. Strategic compassion ensures that your workers will be happy and more productive. Moreover, it allows you to grow as a leader to the extent that the sky is the limit—the more you polish yourself, the more you put into developing your inner strengths, the more valuable you become to your employer. And the happier and more satisfied you become as a working professional.

Millennials have an inherent understanding of this process, though they don't realize what the term strategic compassion means. Some may even feel insulted by it, as if you're manipulating them by "acting" like you care. Well, it won't work if you're "acting." For one thing, people can sense insincerity almost immediately. For another, you can't keep acting like you are sincere 24/7. You'll be exposed one way or another if you're not genuine. And when that happens, whatever trust you've built will come crashing down. Consistency in behavior is what leads to good will, and if your "negative side" is exposed—the one that succumbs to negative emotional triggers—then you'll lose a lot, if not all, of the trust that you had built.

On the other hand, if you mean what you say, then Millennials will respond to you wholeheartedly. They're seeking leadership—whether they see it as surrogate parenting, coaching, or mentoring is irrelevant. If you show that you care, they will respond by working hard. If you give them a clear career path, they will walk that with you side by side. And if you listen to what they have to say and credit them for their successes, you'll have engendered a deep sense of trust that they will, in turn, pass on to the next wave of hires who join your growing business. That's when your company culture takes real root and when your vision is institutionalized as a success.

Leadership is an opportunity to reach your potential and make a huge difference in your life. And by becoming a strong leader you can have a positive influence over the lives of others as well. Real, humanistic leadership can be accomplished by anybody regardless of position, title, or education. The main ingredients to becoming a successful leader are looking past your own troubles or desires by concerning yourself with others. This requires courage and dedication, as well as self-discipline and consideration.

Leadership in management is the key to success itself. It always rests at the top. Take responsibility. You have to tackle yourself first.

Over the next 5–10 years, the majority of people in your company will be Millennials. Ten years flies by in a flash. The math is this simple: to be a relevant commodity, the people who develop humanistic skills and can manage, raise, and inspire this age group are the ones who will be leading their companies. We know this is going to be the case, and so the chance to do this is now. It's critical that you start developing strategically compassionate skills now.

We can look at our rapidly transforming culture in two ways—it's either a crisis, or it's an opportunity to grow. Set aside your business interests for a moment—wouldn't there be outstanding benefits in all aspects of your life to the extent that you develop inner strength, a control over your emotional triggers, and genuine consideration for others? Don't view the ethos of Millennials as a pain; rather this is a great opportunity for you to develop very valuable skills.

One woman I had a chance to work with, Linda, was a rising star at her company. She had been recently promoted and was being groomed for a corporate-level role. She was very smart and could be tough when she needed to be in deal-making. Because of her success and talent she was tasked with growing her team, adding new people and giving existing staff more responsibilities. Linda also had a capacity to genuinely care about people, and she was well liked within the company.

Her experience in leading a large team was limited, however, and she was used to working efficiently on her own. How to successfully lead a large group of people was something she was going to have to learn how to do. Her current team was comprised of Millennials, and they all worked hard. They didn't have a great deal of experience, though, and many times Linda would have to step in to complete projects. We've seen this before—she was so talented that she could do this while also handling her own work. But now that the team was growing, so were her responsibilities.

Linda's style was to point out directly what individuals were doing wrong and what they hadn't done. She was always respectful, but she wouldn't hold back. It was necessary, of course, to expose mistakes, but how she did it wasn't getting the results she wanted. Also a lot of her Millennial team members were starting to ask for promotions (sound familiar?) and yet they still weren't completely delivering on their existing responsibilities. This was extremely frustrating to Linda, who had worked her way up and had earned everything she had. Her natural response was, "Are you kidding me?"

We went to work on how she needed to handle her team in a way that would get the best out of them, keep them happy, and enable her to depend on them to perform as the workload increased. Linda's challenge was to persuade them to see what they needed to improve on and at the same time encourage them to work hard and take responsibility. We began to examine how she approached them when they didn't do something correctly. She started using the problem-solving formula, and making sure in the process that she objectified the issue so they didn't take it personally while still providing them with the knowledge they needed to perform better. She then addressed their desires for a promotion using the steps we outlined for developing a career path.

Keep in mind that Linda was incredibly busy, so she had to take precious time out of her day to do this with several people. But it paid off, because the results were that Linda was able to draw better performance out of all of them and balance out the projects within her team to allow some of them to grow by taking on new responsibilities. Most importantly, in the end, this development gave Linda *more* time to grow her department. Also it clearly relieved some of the stress she was experiencing by feeling that she had to constantly worry whether work was getting done on time and done well. All of this allowed Linda to focus on the big picture and create more success for herself and her company.

This comes back to the principle of putting the time in now to reap the rewards later. Build loyalty so your people have your back and are there when you need them. And develop a compassionate leadership style that allows you and your team to perform at everyone's respective best.

Since developing into a leader is a lot of hard work, how does one rejuvenate himself or herself? You're mentoring all these junior workers, but who's mentoring you? You have to continuously study and know what's going on. Can you even be a good mentor if you don't have one?

Of course you can. For one thing, you can always draw on lessons and experiences that past mentors provided you with. For another, I tell people all the time what they need to do is to study—do your homework, educate yourself about what's new, and learn constantly what other companies are doing. Get to know your industry well, especially if you're in one that's changing.

It's also very useful to familiarize yourself with how Millennials have grown up socially. If you say you've never texted, and you're not familiar with a social media platform (Facebook, Twitter, Instagram, etc.), then you're separating yourself from most everyone else. You need to prioritize educating yourself to become tech savvy. If you don't do it, then you've cut yourself off from an entire generation.

The techniques in this book are almost exclusively directed to how you, as a leader, can best serve your Millennial staff, but let's consider the flip side of that coin as well. How do you best serve your boss—your CEO, the company president, and the corporate entity for which you work in general?

Sometimes people are promoted to important and influential positions, such as a corporate presidency, with no management experience at all. It happens with relative frequency in the entertainment industry, for example. If you suddenly find yourself with a boss like this, what do you do? How do you manage up?

If you're going to your superiors and keep getting a cold shoulder, or if you generally don't have a sense that not getting enough attention, there are few points you ought to consider. For one, if you're spinning 20 plates, they're probably spinning 50. They'll have at least twice the pressure you have, with problems that you don't even know about. They may even be keeping things from you to protect you. If you come at it more from the perspective of being supportive of them, well then that takes pressure off of them and their goals. Now you're not seen as a pest—you're a contributor. You become a supporter.

Every CEO out there runs a business on at least 4 to 5, or at most 10, pillars every year. Even if you're far removed from the CEO, I always encourage people to know where their leader is trying to take the company each respective year. You may have something you want to do, but if it doesn't line up with the boss's pillars, then you may very well be considered a distraction. This doesn't mean that your idea isn't a good one, but timing is everything, and your timing might be off.

Instead, if you're seen as someone overtly supporting the corporate pillars, then you're also viewed as a true contributor. This puts you in tune with where the company's going, so in that context come up with contributive ideas. Your keen perception of such corporate vision allows you to not only look outside your own cubicle but promotes your ability to matrix manage. Don't walk in to the CEO's office asking, or worse whining, about something. Alternatively, when you meet with him or her introduce something that's going to help and contribute to what's very important to the company.

When you're really busy, don't you hate it when someone else insists on complaining to you? It's a huge energy drain. Consider two executives—one is constantly talking about ideas that are viewed as unaligned with the corporate vision, and someone else, even if they're not as capable, is not. Which executive would the CEO want to work with? Who would you prefer?

Here's your ace in the hole with your superiors: If you care about your own security, you should care about your boss's too. If you're looking to move up the ladder, your attitude about where the company's going is critical. Senior managers are always talking about what to do with people who are whining—they're not exactly talking about performance here; they're concerned about attitude.

Different departments or shifts will often blame the other shift for screwing something up. If you bring that up once, well that might be viewed as appropriate. If it happens twice, then an opinion inevitably starts to form that you're trying to undermine others. As the leader of a group pointing fingers outside the group, instruct your people to focus on doing their parts the best they possibly can.

In the long run, employees who constantly complain, or who are not satisfied, or who do everything by pressuring people, show a lack of respect. And, in turn, colleagues don't respect them as well. People who conduct themselves in such a way look like they can't take responsibility. That considerably undermines your ability to be a real leader with authority.

Keep your bosses informed about what's going on, even if you're supportive and working your tail off. Don't make them come looking for you; rather, figure out a way to report consistently about what's going on. Ask them how they'd like to find out from you such information, whether by meetings, memos, e-mails? The point in establishing your relationship with your boss is to be the proactive protagonist.

This is how you become a dependable supporter and the go-to person. If someone has a cooperative relationship with you, he or she is far more likely to give you the new project or opportunity when it comes up. Most people want to work with people they like and get along with, and especially with people they perceive as supporters. Everyone has to deal with job security and insecurity—it should be obvious that you need to have your boss's back. In turn, they won't need to feel that you're holding anything back. And you'll be viewed as a trusted and dependable member of the corporate team.

If you're leading a team please be clear about goals, meet with everyone on a regular basis, know what everyone is responsible for, and step in when someone's not holding up his or her end. In addition, though, you have to keep calling plays. You'll always need something new, to keep things fresh. From time to time, have different people work together, explore ways to be more productive or efficient.

Leadership in the old days went by the now-played-out maxim that when the boss says jump, you say how high. That won't work with Millennials.

Reputation is critical to maintaining leadership. How do you establish a good reputation? When you can control your emotions to the extent that you're someone to be depended on when things go wrong. The person who can control himself or herself under pressure is the sort of person with a good reputation that spreads like wildfire. You're not only solving the problem but you're establishing yourself as a solid leader. No insulting, no shouting, no putting anyone down—people want you. When you start out in a group, the first few moves you make is how you'll be judged. If you start out controlling yourself, you'll be trusted. If you don't, then you trigger everyone else's emotional triggers and you create chaos.

It's very hard to have perspective when your emotional triggers are stimulated. If you're feeling anger, and you feel you're about to explode, remember your trigger word and think—is what you're about to say going to benefit anyone? If not, don't say it. In a sense, truth is useless unless it creates any value.

Let's say you see a very overweight person, and you tell him that it's really unhealthy and unattractive to be obese—that may be the truth, but does this create any value for anyone? No it doesn't, because for one thing it probably just triggers whatever makes this person overeat in the first place. It's just your ego that wants you to say what you think is right. That's being dead right—you've lost because by indulging your ego you've failed to create any value.

CONCLUSION

People, more than anything, want to be happy. We all want to succeed in business, and we all want to earn as much money as we can—However, such success isn't necessarily happiness. As we've seen throughout this book, happiness is not a life without worries or struggles. Happiness, rather, can be sense, the sense of fulfillment one feels when bravely confronting hardship. It is that elevation of the spirit, like an airplane gaining lift from resistance against its wings, that gives people satisfaction and joy. It's perfectly fine to worry and to struggle—that's just part of life, and, in particular, of business. But the kind of happiness I've discussed in this book, and the key to success in business, is the sort of resilient spirit that without complaints or feelings of disaffection allows us to always look on the bright side of a situation and find in it a source of hope.

You will succeed in the 21st-century workplace to the extent that you develop empathy and consideration toward your colleagues and reports. In a nutshell, that's strategic compassion—it's inarguably now in your best interest to behave humanely in your job and to nurture those around you. Yet we've seen how this is viewed by some, still to this day, as a counterintuitive approach to business; the truth is that such behavior now is expected in the American workplace. There is little to be gained by yelling at people, abusing them, or creating insecurity at work by creating a culture of fear.

In August 2015 the *New York Times* published a devastating article describing what it suggested were abusive business practices in the corporate headquarters of Amazon. Whether or not such practices actually occur, it was the reaction to the article that was most intriguing. Amazon was widely denounced, and many people went so far as to say that they'll stop shopping on Amazon as a result of what was reported by the *Times*. And other, smaller tech companies were quoted, gleefully, about how they regularly recruit the best and brightest from Amazon because the recruits prefer to work in their friendlier and supportive environments. If nothing else, the visceral reaction to the *Times* story shows what people today think is not only important but *expected* in a contemporary workplace.

People spend a lot of time at work, and they want to enjoy their lives. Basically, everyone wants to be treated with respect and acknowledged for their efforts. We also want to get along with others the best we can and create work environments that are not hostile or unfriendly. Of course, people wrapped up in anger, greed, or envy don't care about such environments, but they too will have to come to understand that they'll need to change in order to succeed over a longer period of time. People just won't willingly follow or support them.

Of course, most of us also want to "climb the ladder" and become a huge success. So intuitively we want to focus on ourselves and advance without interference by either the people we work for or the people who work for us.

The idea of focusing concern on others in order to become successful may seem the opposite of the type of behavior that will get us to the top. However, as demonstrated by all of the case studies in this book, it's this type of humanistic leadership that will allow you succeed at a *faster* pace than just looking out for yourself and your own goals. The success of the people you lead and your personal success are inextricably tied together. So is your behavior and your environment. Ultimately how you treat and interact with people will net you the same effects or treatment.

You're creating your own environment in any sphere of activity based on your behavior, and how you treat people—whether you're interacting in a business, social, or family environment. Probably one of the reasons Millennials tend to naturally treat all people with respect is that they grew up in a digital, global environment. They could see on their cell phones, and in a moment's notice, the effects of people's actions around the world. They could also establish friendships and interact with people their own age daily, whether they were in Japan, Africa, or Europe. Unless you grew up in the digital age you *do not* have that experience. Accordingly, Millennials have much less apprehension about working with other cultures globally. What does that tell you about the future? If you're successful at leading and managing Millennials, by default you're far more likely to succeed in business in a global environment and economy.

The Millennial generation has pluses and minuses, just as Generation X, and the baby boomer generation had. Complaining about the minuses is just a waste of time. Naturally, you're not going to like a Millennial's attitude when it comes to feeling entitled to a raise or promotion without having earned either. However, when you look at their many positive attributes, such as respecting people, a lack of prejudice, and predilection to work with the people of the world, most would agree that those attributes far outweigh the negative ones.

As we say in Buddhism, obstacles turn into benefits if they allow you to grow as a leader and as a human being. By growing as a leader yourself, you will be able to see through the superficial actions of people that do not create value and get to the true reason for their behavior. Making this effort will allow them to trust you, and, in turn, you can get them to perform far better at their jobs. By accomplishing this, your life will greatly improve as your stress levels drop because you can now trust *them* to support you, communicate what's going on, and take responsibility for what they need to accomplish. Now you can focus on growing your department and expanding your responsibilities.

For many of us, the key to unlocking our potentials to lead the Millennials on their terms is control of our emotional triggers. Anger can be a great motivator for energy and effort, but when we lose control of our emotions there will be trouble—especially in a Millennial context. You've got to build a solid self. Not only will that advance your career, but it will help you transform into a happier individual. Controlling emotional triggers and learning how to communicate are the primary skills that lead toward excellent leadership. For whatever reason, these two elements were perhaps the least emphasized of business skills in past generations, so the change in business mores over the past 10 years or so is breathtaking. But like all good businesses, and businesspersons, we have to adapt. More than anything, get a hold of yourself and learn how to express yourself clearly and in an encouraging and inspiring way.

As we've seen, workers today will not be motivated by shouting and fear. Especially at the most desirable of positions, such as engineering, people will simply leave for another company. There's no sense of false loyalty to any corporation; rather, Millennials (and others) will simply go where they're most appreciated. On the other hand, your reports will run through walls for you if they know that you care for them, if you're inclusive, and if you genuinely appreciate their efforts.

This is the new culture of corporate leadership in America. As important as it is to business to achieve an MBA, or to at least understand how business works, it's now equally as vital to appreciate the transforming psychology of the contemporary workplace. And, more than that, it's critical that you put these new mores into play as Millennials further dominate the workplace, all the way up to the highest executive levels.

I trust that the information and techniques presented in this book will open up new doors for you on your path to becoming a happy and humanistic leader who will build a profitable and successful future for you and your company. Your success and happiness—more than ever—are entirely dependent on your insights, internal transformation, and sincerity to care about those with whom you work.

Appendix
Millennial Generation Facts and Figures[1]

- Millennials (those born after 1980) are America's most racially diverse generation. Some 43 percent of Millennial adults are nonwhite, the highest share of any generation.
- Half of Millennials (50%) describe themselves as political independents and about 3 in 10 (29%) say they are not affiliated with any religion.
- Only 26 percent of this generation is married. When they were the age that Millennials are now, 48 percent of baby boomers were married. The median age at first marriage is now the highest in modern history—29 for men and 27 for women.
- Eighty-one percent of Millennials are on Facebook, where their generation's median friend count is 250, far higher than that of older age groups. Fifty-five percent have posted a "selfie" on a social media site. Only about 6 in 10 boomers say they know what a "selfie" is (it's a photo taken of oneself).
- Nineteen percent of Millennials say most people can be trusted, compared with 40 percent of boomers.
- Forty-nine percent of Millennials say the country's best years are ahead, a view held by 44 percent of boomers.
- Millennials are the first generation in the modern era to have higher levels of student loan debt, poverty and unemployment, and lower levels of wealth and personal income than their two immediate predecessor generations (Gen Xers and boomers) had at the same stage of their life cycles.

- A third of older Millennials (ages 26 to 33) have a four-year college degree or more—making them the best-educated cohort of young adults in American history.
- Two-thirds of recent bachelor's degree recipients have outstanding student loans, with an average debt of about $27,000. Two decades ago, only half of recent graduates had college debt, and the average was $15,000.
- In 2012, 47 percent of births to women in the Millennial generation were nonmarital. In 1996, just 35 percent of births were outside of marriage.
- More than 8 in 10 say they either currently have enough money to lead the lives they want (32%) or expect to have in the future (53%).
- Half of Millennials (51%) say they do not believe there will be any money for them in the Social Security system by the time they are ready to retire.
- Only about half (49%) of Millennials say the phrase "a patriotic person" describes them very well. By contrast, 75 percent of boomers say this describes them very well.
- Millennials are also somewhat less likely than older adults to describe themselves as environmentalists—just 32 percent say this describes them very well, compared with at least 4 in 10 among all older generations.

NOTE

1. Information included in this Appendix is derived from the Pew Research Foundation's February 2014 survey on Millennial generation trends, available at http://www.pewsocialtrends.org/2014/03/07/millennials-in-adulthood/

Index

Acknowledgment, 20, 59, 63–66, 87–89
Adaptability, 58, 115
Adversity, inner strength and, 81–82
Aggression, insecurity in, 79
Amazon, 122
Anger: controlling, 26, 46, 123; impact of, 29–32; leadership and, 10–11; listening and, 44; of middle managers, 36–38; respect defusing, 42–43
Apollo 13 (film), 77
Appreciation, expressing, 93
Aristotle, 10, 82
The Art of War (Sun Tzu), 78

Blame, solution vs., 4–5
Branson, Richard, 2, 51, 68
Buddhahood, 64
Buddhism: applied to business, 16; compassion and, 14, 40; dependent origination and, 21, 40, 116; facing weakness and, 26–29; hierarchy of life in, 75–76, 97; mentoring in, 99
Business: compassion and, 40; leadership in, 10–11, 14–15; Machiavellian approach, 74–75; mentoring in, 17, 100–101; as warfare, 74–75, 78

Career paths: developing, 38–39, 44–45, 118; strategic plan for, 112–13
Challenger explosion, 4
Change, resistance to, 99
Clinton, Bill, 113
Clooney, George, 109
Communication: of company/team goals, 112–13; consistency and, 68, 69; developing skills in, 90–91; directness/honesty in, 107–9; empathy and, 35–36, 65, 106; expressing gratitude, 106–7; follow up and, 110–11; leadership and, 123; learning effective, 39, 105; listening and, 106–7; proactivity and, 109–10; of set standards, 111–12
Competition, Machiavellian approach to, 74–75
Complainers: acknowledging, 20–21; effect of, 7, 119–20
Consideration: lack of, 33–35; leadership and, 2–5, 9–11, 66–68; Millennials expecting, 18–19
Consistency, 60, 68, 69, 90, 96, 110
Cooperation, 5, 89, 120
Corporate culture: benefits of, 102–4; challenges to, 97–99; consistency/

trust in, 96–97; creating open, 96; examples of, 102; mentoring in, 99–101; negative, 97; overview of, 95–96; succession planning in, 101–2
Corporate values, 51–52
Cost, of employee turnover, 8–9, 31
Coworker negativity, 7, 73–74
Crises: good leadership and, 59–60; as opportunities, 52; staying focused in, 76–77
Criticism, 19, 66, 98

Dalai Lama, 41, 79
Dependent origination, 21, 40, 116
Drucker, Peter, 55

Education, executive, 17
Emotional intelligence quotient (EQ), 1–2, 51
Emotional triggers: controlling, 26–29, 43, 73–74, 82, 123; example of, 29–32; explanation of, 23; leading meetings and, 91–92; list of, 24; pushback and, 80–81, 120–21; respect defusing, 42–43; understanding, 25–26
Empathy: in acknowledging upsets, 59; in communication, 35–36, 65, 106; lack of, 33–35; leadership and, 2–5, 9–11, 66–68, 121; in Millennials, 40; personal history and, 6; productivity and, 8–9
Employee turnover, 8–9
Encouragement, 3–4
Enron, 54
Environment, 93, 96. *See also* Humanistic environment
EQ (emotional intelligence quotient), 1–2, 51
Ethos, 10
Executive education, 17

Fiddler on the Roof, 29
Flying Tigers air cargo line, 103
Follow-up, 110–11

Google, 68, 96, 102
Gratitude, 93, 106–7

Happiness, essence of, 121
Harris, Ed, 77
Hierarchy of life, 75–76, 97
Hsieh, Tony, 51
Human experience, Buddhist view of, 75–76
Humanistic environment: importance of, 3; performance and, 6–7, 10–11; successful business and, 14

Identification, of problems, 4–5
Ikeda, Daisaku, 64
Inner strength: adversity and, 81–82; developing, 78–79; during pushback, 80–81
Insecurity, aggression and, 79
Insincerity, 8, 116
Integrity, 60–61
Intrinsic value, 64

Johnson, Robert Wood, II, 54
Johnson & Johnson, 53–54

Knowledge worker, 55
Kranz, Gene, 77

Law firm management, 53
Lay, Kenneth, 47
Leadership: abusive, 33–34; in business context, 10–11, 14–15; calm in crises, 76–77; consistency and, 68, 69; empathy and, 2–5, 9–11, 66–68, 121; finding/developing, 50; good reputation and, 120–21; high EQ and, 1–2; humanistic, 13–14, 18–19, 50–51; integrity and, 60–61; management vs., 7, 16, 49–55; of Millennials, 52–54, 58, 123–24; proactivity in, 109–10; qualities of, 49, 52–53; sincerity in, 8–9; successful, example of, 59–60, 103; team building and, 55; trust in, 48; unsuccessful, example of, 56–57

Listening skills: defusing anger, 44; for effective communication, 106–7; importance of, 36; leading meetings and, 85–89, 91–92
Logos, 10, 44–45

Ma, Jack, 47
Machiavelli, Niccolo, 74–75, 79
Management: delegating and, 66–67; insincere, 8; instead of criticism, 66; of law firms, 53; leadership vs., 2, 7, 16, 49–55; matrix, 46; toxic, 7–8
Management Challenges in the 21st Century (Drucker), 55–56
Mandela, Nelson, 51
Matrix management, 46, 48
Meetings: acknowledging everyone, 87–89; emergency, 93–94; emotional triggers and, 90–92; inefficient, 83; learning to lead, 85–87; steps for successful, 84, 92–93; trust building at, 90
Mentoring, 17–18, 99–101, 112
Mid-level managers: communication skills and, 36–38; difficulties of, 35; successful, example of, 57–58
The Midnight Special, 14
Millennials: advocating for, 36–38; characteristics of, 11–12, 21; developing career paths for, 38–39, 44–45, 118; empathy in, 40; expecting respect, 18–19, 122; leadership of, 51, 52–54, 58, 115–17, 123–24; mentoring of, 99–101; motivation of, 63–64; shortcomings of, 44; understanding, 118
Money, as motivator, 63
Motivation, 63–64
Musk, Elon, 77–78

New hires, supporting, 69
New York Times, 121–22
Nichiren Daishonin, 76
Nonverbal communication, 106

O'Leary, Kevin, 74
Opportunity, crisis as, 52
Optimism, 11

Pathos, 10
Patton, General George, 50
Paypal, 77–78
People: investing in, 101; as resources, 33–34, 40, 64–65
PEP (productivity, efficiency, and performance), 2, 10
Performance: EQ and, 2; humanistic environment and, 6–7; sincerity and, 8–9
Personal history, understanding, 6, 19, 36
Pessimism, 11
Political maneuvering, 33–35, 75, 96
Positive pressure, 3–4
Praise, 66, 73, 106–7
Prescott, Bob, 103
Present moment, 16
The Prince (Machiavelli), 74
Proactive leadership, 109–10
Problem solving, solution approach to, 4–5
Productivity: humanistic leadership and, 19–21, 59–60; mentoring increasing, 18; sincerity and, 8–9; toxic managers and, 7
Productivity, efficiency, and performance (PEP), 2, 10
Pushback: inner strength and, 78–81; staying focused, 75–77

Reality, Millennials and, 44–45
Reassurance, 5, 106
Relationships, 9–10
Resources, people as, 33–34, 40, 64–65
Respect: defusing anger, 42–43; expectation of, 122; Millennials expecting, 18–19, 122
Responsibility, 3–4, 7, 43, 67
Rock, David, 63
Root cause of problems, 4–5, 58

SAS Institute, 68–69
Savings, of humanistic leadership, 19–21
Schwartz, Jeffry, 63
Schwartz, Morrie, 26
Scott, George C., 50
Self-control, of emotional triggers, 26–29, 43, 73–74, 82, 123
Seligman, Martin, 11
Shyness: overcompensating for, 90–91; support for, 88–89
Sincerity, 8–9, 21, 116
Society for Human Resources Management (SHRM), 9
Solution approach, to problem solving, 4–5
Space Exploration Technologies (SpaceX), 77
Spitzer, Eliot, 33–34
Steinbrenner, George, 7
Strategic compassion: aggression vs., 79; emotional triggers and, 43–44; explanation of, 41–42; inner strength and, 78–79; Millennials and, 44–45, 115–17; proactivity and, 109–10; problem workers and, 73–74; productivity and, 19–21, 59–60, 116; rewards of, 47, 117–18; skill of, 50–51; in successful leadership, 121–22; with superiors, 118–20; support in, 69–70; trust in, 48
Strategic planning, 112–13
Strengths, Weaknesses, Opportunities, and Threats (SWOT) analysis, 17–18, 66, 68, 106, 111
Strong-arming, 33–34
Succession planning, 101–2
Sullenberger, Chesley, 77
Sun Tzu, 78
Support: importance of, 69–70; for superiors, 118–20

Team building, 3–4, 28, 53, 55
Team meetings. *See* Meetings
Technical expertise, 118
Ten Worlds, 75–76, 97
Tesla Motors, 77–78
T'ien-T'ai (Zhiyi), 75–76
Toughness, proper use of, 64–65
Toxic coworkers, 7, 42, 73–74
Toxic managers, 7–8
Trigger words, 4, 28–29, 32, 43–44
Trump, Donald, 40
Trust: in dealing with anger, 46; developing, 8, 9, 19–20; leadership and, 48, 53; in open culture, 97; at team meetings, 90

Up In the Air! (film), 109

Virgin Atlantic airlines, 2, 51, 68

Warfare, business as, 74–75, 78
Weakness, 26–29, 79
Wegmans supermarkets, 69
Workplace satisfaction, 63–64

Zappos, 51–52
Zhiyi (T'ien-T'ai), 75–76

About the Author

MARC ROBERTSON is the founder of Los Angeles–based New Skills USA (newskills.us.com) and has more than 25 years of experience in the media, entertainment, and technology industries. Marc has successfully coached leaders, executives, and managers utilizing emotional intelligence quotient, environmental awareness, leadership skills, and business acumen. All of his coaching is based on solving actual problems and issues that the respective individual currently faces.

Marc has a strong track record working with developing companies and guiding executives to develop a humanistic and results-orientated leadership style. His clients include SpaceX, DirecTV, Intel, Live Nation, and Qualcomm. His industry positions have included CEO, COO, and executive vice president. Marc holds an MBA from Loyola Marymount University ("LMU"), an AMP Certificate from IESE Business School in Spain, and a BA in communication arts from LMU.